WHO'S ON YOUR DREAM TEAM?

PALMETTO
PUBLISHING
Charleston, SC
www.PalmettoPublishing.com

Who's On Your Dream Team?
Copyright © 2023 by Irvin G. Schorsch III

Hardcover ISBN: 978-1-962045-01-8
Paperback ISBN: 978-1-962045-02-5
eBook ISBN: 978-1-962045-00-1
audio: 978-1-962045-03-2

Who's On Your

DREAM TEAM?

How to Find a Fiduciary Committed to Your Family and Your Ever Changing Life

By Irvin G. Schorsch III

With Ted Spiker

TABLE OF CONTENTS

Introduction

REIMAGINE YOUR FINANCES AND YOUR FUTURE

The secret to achieving your financial goals, realizing your dreams, and living a happier life comes down to one simple choice:

What do you want out of life? See if you agree with this list:

- A life that's financially secure and prosperous.
- A life that lets you pursue your passions.
- A life that allows you to work with a fulfilling purpose.
- A life that gives you the time and space to laugh and love, dance and dream, create and care about the people around you.
- A life that matters.

Instead don't your days feel anything but that?

We have money stresses, we have health struggles, we have family angst (wait, I spent how much on college tuition and now Freddy wants to move back in with us?). We wake up and don't know which way is up between the state of current affairs and our lack of faith in leaders to guide us through them. And frankly every minute seems like it's spent solving something, working on something, stressing over something—and not doing anything we really want.

Honestly some days it can feel like you've got a tractor trailer parked in your heart, a cactus pinballing in your brain, and a six-eyed monster tormenting your intestines with worry, anxiety, and fear.

So what do you do when life doesn't work? You flounder, get frustrated, bounce from project to project, and feel stuck. But are we really stuck? I say a resounding no.

The answer is simple: find the right kind of fiduciary who can be your trusted partner in your mission to:

- Lower your anxiety
- Lighten your conflicts
- Solve nagging problems
- Elevate your joy
- Give you back your time to do what you most want
- Increase your wealth

This book is about helping you find a reputable and family-oriented fiduciary that can help you conquer your battles and get you out of the frustrating mazes of life that seem to have walls blocking every way out.

This is the answer that can calm your heart, ease your mind, and take that pit out of your stomach and toss it right down the garbage disposal.

While one of the goals of fiduciaries is to increase your bottom line, here's my bottom line:

Fiduciaries should serve you and your family by helping you examine all the moving pieces of your life through the lens of money and finance *and* help you overcome the stumbling blocks you encounter from week to week, month to month, and year to year. With that partnership, you can take back your time, reengage in your passions, and lead the life that you want.

It's incredible, actually. Not only should these firms talk about dollars and cents, but they should also live in your back pocket as your ultimate Swiss Army knife of life: they—and their network of people they partner with—should serve as part financial planner, part mental-health counselor, part coach, part family therapist, part negotiator, part lawyer, part accountant, part confidante, part friend, and a zillion other roles they can serve in your pursuit of a better life.

This isn't just about making money; earning money is no fun if you can't pair up the money with freeing up the time to do what you want. Indeed I want people to feel like this: when you wake up, you're excited to go into the world, because you love what you do, you can enjoy your money, you have the time to explore your passions with the people you love, and you have a clear purpose for your life.

This book will help get you there—through the stumbling blocks of life as they happen.

In my line of work, I tell it to my clients straight—no sugarcoating, no fluff, no letting them bury their heads in the sand when the shizzle hits the fan.

After my 30 plus years in the wealth management industry and getting a ringside seat to some serious struggles, I know that, for most of us, life is a 12-round prize fight. And when we're not prepared for what's coming, we stand to get sucker punched by one of life's no-good knuckles.

Yes, we all want to (and should) celebrate the blissful euphoria that comes with such joys as the birth of a child, a dream job, or an Instagram-worthy sunset. But we also must be armored against the lows, the conflicts, the worries, the uncertainties, and the fact that you—right this very second—can practically feel your stress hormones oozing out of your eyeballs.

Does this sound familiar?

You never have enough hours to do everything you want, so you feel you're swirling in a whirlpool of compromises—sacrificing your time, passions, and energy to keep working and keep trudging to get from the start of the day to the end of it. And then, bam, a major life event occurs…

You find out that Aunt Tilly's Parkinson's is getting worse, and you feel like you're the only family member who can or wants to help. *Wait, she wants to move in?!*

Your kids are sputtering with their own issues, and you feel frustrated that you can't fix them the way you could when they were toddlers. *Wait, THEY want to move back home?!*

You read or watch the news, and you have no confidence that our leaders will do anything to help. *What's this world coming to?*

You have spent so much of the last two years worrying about and adapting to Covid disruptions, and you seem to encounter a new fight every day. *Oh no, here we go again.*

You need to work more when you truly just long to work less. *Honey, when is it going to stop? When is life going to get better???*

So your mind races like an Indy 500 driver all the time (and there's not a pit stop in sight!). How can you take back your time, care for your family, and not spend every stinking second worrying about your future? And for the love of all things holy, wouldn't it be nice to actually play tennis for the first time since Walter Cronkite was on the air?

Here's the really scary thing. You may have spent years—even decades—grinding along, not thinking about or planning for your future, or perhaps not doing it as well or as thoroughly as you wished you had. When you think about that scary scenario, your angst feels like it quadruples.

Maybe you even feel like a human rubber band, and everyone wants to grab a piece of you and pull you in a different direction. You feel tired, alone, and virtually depleted of your former you.

And then you…

Snap.

Even the strongest of fighters can't withstand all the tension we face in life.

If you feel like you're alone in the ring with no end to the fight in sight, then you've come to the substance of what I'm here to unpack in this book.

You can reclaim your freedom, rethink your fiscal and familial strategies, and reimagine your life.

Dreams. Passions. Joys. Time.

After all, wouldn't your life feel a whole lot better if it were less of a fight and more of a dance—gliding in unison with your partner and loved ones so that you can bathe in those joys, laughs, and love?

The reason I wrote this book is because I want to help you change your narrative and mindset to help you get ahead. After all, the old way of thinking about money—work hard and save!—just doesn't cut it anymore. Life is too complicated today to simply hope that "stuff will work out."

Who's On Your Dream Team? is indeed about money, finance, and wealth, but it's not about the nuts and bolts of investment strategies, stocks and bonds, or compound interest (though they're all important). Those strategies are available in my first book, *Reinvent Rich, How to Make More Money, More Moments and More Meaning in Life.* This book is about deploying a secret weapon in your battle to reclaim time and freedom.

Who's On Your Dream Team? will cover such topics as what you should expect from a fiduciary, the benefits you should receive, how to find one you can trust, how to differentiate them from big-box wealth-management firms, as well as other strategies that firms like ours have used to help our clients survive and thrive in their financial and familial lives. Using my 30 plus years of seeing successes (and witnessing the most common mistakes that people make), you can save yourself years of anguish as mistakes linger or worsen and use our experience to help you help yourself.

After all while we rely on experts to navigate certain technicalities of life (doctors, lawyers, mechanics), many of us try to take on our financial and related conflicts by ourselves.

Experts agree that stress around our financial lives is the major issue facing families today. The following quote from the CFP Board says it all. "According to a Capital One survey, more than three-quarters of Americans (77%) reported feeling anxious about their financial situation in January 2020. Since then, financial experts report that consumers' financial stress has only gotten worse due to the global pandemic and subsequent record-level inflation, the latter of which ranked as a top stressor for 87% of Americans." Certified Financial Planner Board® (https://www.cfp.net/knowledge/industry-insights/2022/06/how-the-psychology-of-financial-planning-can-benefit-your-clients-and-your-practice)

Let's be clear. I'm not talking about simply having a personal wealth adviser or someone assigned to pump up your portfolio. Your life—and the complexities that come with it—is bigger than a one-mission job.

A reputable and client-centered fiduciary will act on *your* behalf with your interests always coming first. It is an individual or team that should serve as your advocate in all areas of your life (some of these areas may surprise you), a trusted partner who's almost like a family member (though we never expect a dinner invite), and your teammate who holds up a mirror to your life (so you can take a good look at your own values) when it comes to creating the freedom and leverage that you need and deserve.

After I explain the functions and advantages of fiduciaries, I'll also take you through the most common financial problems I see from our clients, provide some insight into how to tackle them yourself, and then show you how an experienced fiduciary can handle them so you don't have to.

Yes, a key part of our job is to help you make more money, but more vitally we're here to help you leverage your financial picture and successes so you can do with your life exactly what you want, when you want, and how you want.

This book is all about making *your* life better.

How? By reclaiming more of every day to do what you want—and have the money and freedom to do so.

So You Think You Already Have a Fiduciary?

Maybe you already have an investment adviser or work with someone who's classified as a fiduciary. But not all fiduciaries or advisers are alike—and they often function differently, as you'll see throughout this book. Here's a good litmus test to see if yours is being used to the fullest extent possible to help protect you and your family in the best and most holistic way possible.

Does yours have a team of professionals you can choose to work with, rather than one contact person?

Does yours offer a professional network of experts who can be called upon no matter what your problem or question.

Does yours have more than 100 combined years of background and experience to draw upon?

Does yours change goals and advice customized to you as your life evolves?

Does yours do more than just make recommendations but rather teach you how to think?

Does yours use innovative techniques—like mind maps—to help you create a vision for you and your family?

If the answer is "no" to the majority of those questions, then you may not be getting the most out of your advisers.

Chapter 1

WHO ARE YOU?

**If you want even more out of life,
you've come to the right place.**

What do you want right now?

Whatever your answer—*more sleep! a better job! that $4.99 all-you-can-eat nacho special!*—I certainly can't know exactly what lies at the other end of my question.

But if you've made the literary leap from the Introduction to Chapter 1, then I can take a stab at some things that may make you tick.

You care about your wealth and your family's future.

You care about taking care of yourself and providing for others.

You care about "what's next" because you care about "what's important."

You care about the things that matter most in life.

But I'll take another stab here. You're also here because life isn't easy. In fact it's more complicated than a 5,000-piece, all-white jig-saw puzzle.

You have conflicts. You have pressures. You have things in life that confuse you. You have people in life who infuriate you. You have a dumpster fire's worth of problems to handle. And it certainly feels like you have close to zero time in your life to address all of it.

Here's the crazy thing. These problems aren't exclusive to any one demographic. They happen to everyone—albeit a bit differently.

If you're a millennial, you may be in the early stages of your career, trying to build your wealth, managing the pressures of life (and the additional ones coming out of a pandemic), and dealing with a whole lot of stuff. After all, your generation has been inundated with mental-health challenges (including serious ones involving addiction) and a rapidly changing professional environment linked to technological advances. It's not easy finding your way and carving out your path in life.

If you're smack dab in the middle of life, you have your own set of issues. Yes, perhaps you've established a very nice career and nest egg, and you've grown into knowing who you are and what you want. But this is the time of life when you see what's behind door number 2 and it's not always pretty. You can be greeted with a jambalaya peppered with all kinds of seemingly insurmountable ingredients: health problems, college tuition, aging parents, job uncertainty, family strife, broken marriages, and Wi-Fi connections that are less stable than a two-legged table. Any of it can be maddening, but life gets even more complicated when several major issues collide at once.

If you're near or entering retirement, you may worry about having enough money or having health issues you're tackling. You wonder what your future is going to be, but you have a generation or two behind you that you're also wanting to help—because after all, as the matriarch or patriarch of the family, you want to provide relief to the people experiencing the problems of your extended family.

The point is your challenges at different stages of life may change, but the fact that you will have challenges never changes.

The key, in my mind, is that self-determined people—people who can calmly and creatively choose their path—have the best chance of surviving the rough waters and metaphorically or literally landing on the idyllic beach of their dreams.

You hold the power to your own success.

And there are people who can help you. That's where we come in. We come in to give you one thing that you can't buy on Amazon: *time.*

Time creates money.

Time creates freedom.

Time creates the power to create the life you want.

And all I want is to help you do just that.

That's what this book is about—no matter who you are, no matter your financial status, no matter your challenges, no matter your dreams, no matter what your today looks like, and no matter what your *tomorrow* looks like.

After all, the people who do best in life aren't the ones who think they can do it all themselves. They're the ones who are wise and self-determined enough to know that they can't.

Chapter 2

THE PERFECT PARTNERSHIP

The roles and responsibilities of fiduciaries in your life will give you a glimpse into how they can help you navigate life's turbulent times.

A world-renowned surgeon has two special, secluded homes off the coast of Maryland, and his wife owns many, many artistic masterpieces. Sounds idyllic, doesn't it?

What if I told you that they didn't have enough money to pay their bills? Sounds sort of crazy.

This problem actually isn't that unusual.

The doctor makes a lot of money, and as is the case with many high earners, that money is spent. The family lives beyond their means, enjoying the riches of, well, their riches. In this case Daniel loved their secluded beach front home that was right off the coast, where the views of the water were breathtaking. Ruth spent the money that came in on high-end art (like sketches and drawings from Monet and Prendergast) as well as a unique collection of Japanese linens. And she had a small barn near their property where she kept all the items.

Unfortunately they couldn't find an answer to their financial pain points—that is actually having trouble making ends meet, though they were consistent about establishing and maintaining retirement funds.

I met with the couple to help them look at the problem. The more I listened, the more I realized the tension and their predicament. It was all about the artwork.

"These are like my children," Ruth told me. "Each one is like a baby. They mean so much to me." And she burst into tears.

Now you can imagine why it became such a struggle in the relationship between the couple: How does one person say to another that in order to get the finances straightened out, some of your babies need to be sold off?

That's where a fiduciary can come in.

Something had to give, and I knew what it was. We had to perform emotional surgery, and it took a delicate hand.

We had to separate the asset types from the emotion and solve the income-expense ratio. If I'm looking at the situation objectively, I can see that the beach home was important to keep as it could be enjoyed by the family and would eventually be passed down to their children. The art? There were hundreds of pieces, and I thought we could discuss parting with a handful of the more valuable items to recreate the balance and diversification of assets and create the needed income.

When I met with Ruth, I told her, "I think it's worth your time to sleep on this idea. Ask yourself what's more important—your children's future or parting with a few artistic treasures that give you so much pleasure? And if you are game, we could take high-quality photographs of each piece of art and have them framed to hang on your walls."

And that worked. Months later, she agreed, and we figured out how to do it. I contacted two reputable auction firms (Sotheby's and Christie's), and we arranged to have them look at the pieces in my office (Ruth was so private, she didn't want strangers coming to her home or personal space).

After some front-end work, here's where we landed: we placed several pieces of her art into auction twice—the first round netted $580,000, and the second landed $775,000. I also negotiated away the sell-side commission (buyers paid the buyer's premium), and that gave the family the much-needed cash. Win-win.

While we always advise people to find areas to cut their expenses (that's a tactic that always works), the family couldn't quite get it done.

So what did we do? We acted the way a strong fiduciary does in multiple facets: we were an advocate for their family. We had difficult conversations and managed conflict between the husband and wife (yes, we mediate between husband and wife as well). We interacted with the auction houses and helped with the examination of the art and transportation of the fine art to New York (with the proper insurance). We were a negotiator when it came to the terms of the transaction and commission, and we found a solution that worked for everyone. Ruth passed away shortly after, and Daniel also gifted the vacation home to his children. He now has a strong nest egg to pay for his retirement, and we interacted with his adult offspring to create the appropriate understanding of the parents' gifting intentions.

That result, I'd argue, doesn't happen if you simply have a traditional financial adviser or no one at all. Daniel and Ruth needed us to whack through the bushes of life to find the clear path.

That's the kind of thing a fiduciary can do, and you will read about many more examples and stories throughout this book.

In the end what you're looking for is a fiduciary who can give you these four freedoms*:

- Freedom of time
- Freedom of money
- Freedom of relationships
- Freedom of purpose

*Dan Sullivan and Strategic Coach ® https://www.strategiccoach.com/

To start us off, let's look at some of the key strategies that fiduciaries follow:

We have a duty of loyalty. That means we put a client's interests above the interests of anyone else, including our own firm. That's one of the main ways we're different from large wealth management firms: we don't create or offer commission-based products, which would—by definition—put firm interests over client interests. This loyalty is the main driver of everything we do and guides all of our decisions. That means we avoid conflicts of interest—financial or otherwise--and disclose all potential conflicts. We do what is best for you. Period.

We have a duty to help clients reach their goals. That means we act with care and skill to help clients attain their desires, taking into consideration things like a client's risk tolerance, experience level, time horizons to important goals, and their personal financial situation. We can advise, we can help, we can present all sides of how to handle a scenario, but the client makes the final life decisions.

We have a duty to act with integrity. Acting with integrity is multifaceted, of course, but ultimately it means that we act within ethical guidelines. We are clear and truthful about our advice and information, we develop next steps, and if we don't know answers, we inform our clients and then connect them with people who can help. We make sure we align our actions with our core values, always keeping clients' interests first. It also means we're truthful sharing the positive and negative with our clients, making sure they know the whole picture, not telling them something just because it may be what they want to hear.

With these values we aim to build trust and build a long-lasting partnership.

This partnership allows us to help clients realize their dreams. It's a tricky and confusing world out there—and many folks simply don't have the desire, skill, or patience to handle all of the financial and logistical complexities within their families or their business that get thrown their way. And that's why we're here.

You know, one of the things I tell my clients is that part of the reason we can be so useful is that we're here to teach you not to make the dumb mistakes that others do.

After all, we've seen just about all of them.

And we know the solutions that can get you out of your everyday and long-term pickles.

Life doesn't come with an instruction manual, but we can sure make it feel like it does.

Chapter 3

SUPER POWERS

The life-changing benefits that come from choosing the right fiduciary.

If you look at all the people you regularly work with as part of your personal life, your VIP list probably looks a lot like everyone else's: you have doctors, a dentist, maybe a mechanic you like, maybe an accountant or lawyer, perhaps a barber or stylist, and most definitely the best darn pet sitter to take care of Brutus and Penelope.

You may even have someone you work with on your portfolios and investments, but chances are you don't have a fiduciary or even know much of what we do.

We need to change that.

Because a family focused fiduciary can change *you*.

Shall we count the ways? First and foremost a strong fiduciary will always be your advocate and will commit to being your advocate for the long term. That means your fiduciary will help you develop a process for establishing your financial and life goals—and develop systems and a blueprint for you to reach those goals.

No matter your specific goal, the fiduciary will likely revolve around The Four Freedoms I referred to earlier:

- Freedom of time
- Freedom of money
- Freedom of relationships
- Freedom of purpose

We need to be clear that we're not just talking about making as much money as you can (though that's a foundational piece, for sure). It's also about solving conflicts, making tough decisions, and even stepping in as the world's most underrated marriage and/or family counselor (if needed!).

Let's look at some of the official and unofficial roles of a high-quality fiduciary—and ultimately how one will benefit you.

Interrogator. No, no, no. We're not here to unlock your deep, dark secrets, though you do need to be straightforward about your habits, behaviors, dreams, and stumbling blocks. But our first order of business is to do a deep dive into the business of you.

What do you want?

Strike that.

What do you *really* want?

To get to that answer, we will ask more questions than your favorite TV detective. The fact is we can't do our best work until we know a lot about you. It's not about what we think. It's about what you want. And our initial discovery meetings—as well as our lasting relationship—will get us there. So be ready to open up and speak up. That's where the real foundation begins. Coincidentally I tell our clients it will take 12 to 24 months for us to really understand what makes your life tick.

Connector. One of our main values is this: if we don't know the answer to a question you have or if we don't have the expertise to complete a project, we will find the person or firm who can help you. We are a professional connector, helping you meet up with everyone from accountants, estate attorneys, paperwork organizers, monthly bill payers, and more. (This is the subject of Chapter 6.) This is something you don't get with just a financial adviser, but it is something you get with a fiduciary firm or a family office. We don't pass the buck. It's not "figure it out yourself." It's "we will figure out the many parts needed together" as that is our mission.

Negotiator. While some people like the situations in life that call for cat-and-mouse, poker-face negotiations, other people don't like the process or don't have the time or skill for it. That's where we can come in. Remember the fact that we negotiated away a commission for the art-loving Ruth I talked about in Chapter 2? Well you don't have to have high-end art collections for us to be helpful. We have negotiated such things as lines of credit, mortgage rates, airplane leases, sales of homes, and the costs of moving a loved one into a continuing care retirement community. We very commonly negotiate car acquisitions. In all cases we do our research and work in the interest of our clients to save them money. And we also work to figure out the best possible financing on these purchases, such as whether it's in your best interest to lease, use the bank's money, take the car dealership's loan offer, or negotiate a lower cash deal.

Money Maker. I'll take a deeper dive into the financial aspect of this in Chapter 8. Though this book is not just about investment strategies or financial savviness, it is worth mentioning that, of course, one of our main responsibilities is to help you hit your financial goals. One of my favorite stories revolves around Jerry, a computer programmer who had about $120,000 saved for retirement when we met him (this was about 20 years before his planned retirement). Jerry was single with no kids, and he received about $120,000 from his sister. He said his goal was to get to about $500,000 to $600,000 to achieve his retirement dreams.

We helped Jerry significantly expand that goal.

Note that I said "helped," because Jerry did his part. He lived within his means and his budget, and he did what we advised when it came to saving, investing and spending. And then we were able to do our part in developing his proper asset allocation, dollar cost averaging strategy, use of pretax savings tools and estate planning techniques. The result was a sizable nest egg for his retirement. Now he has the funds he needs to do what he wants. He loves to travel. And even better, he can now offer to his friends to pay their way if they can't afford to go on the trip together with him. It's a win-win. Jerry gets travel companions and gets the joy of helping others, and his friends get to experience life in ways they may not have been able to afford before.

Make no mistake: good fiduciaries also have great financial sense—and don't sell you on their own products or services. They develop investment strategies and monitor them to ensure a solid, sustainable investment return over time.

Traffic Cop. Jonathan and Sarah had one heck of a mess. They were a big, tight family—with all seven of their kids coming over with their own families most every Friday night for a large family dinner together. They spent most every holiday all together. They played games. They laughed. They loved each other. They were together in every sense of the word. But troubled times can hit hard, as they do for so many families.

One of their grandkids had more than $100,000 in college loans and was on the verge of bankruptcy with the added problem of a serious health crisis. Another one of Jonathan's and Sarah's kids (not the parents of this child) wanted to borrow money to buy a small bakery business, but he didn't have the seed money to get started.

The problem: How do we help those in need (or those in want) while being fair to the rest of the family?

Is this something you take to a financial representative? Not likely.

Is this something you could take to a fiduciary with whom you've built a long-lasting relationship? Absolutely.

I got to work. I spoke to creditors chasing the family to help negotiate the student debt down to $65,000. And then Jonathan and Sarah stepped in; they paid the debt off and paid the fees for health services, and they also funded the small business. But what about the fairness part?

We decided to make those payments not as an outright gift, but as a loan against their inheritance. So in that approach the inheritance remained equitable among all seven kids. And the best part is that we can track that for them—down to the penny—to know what was spent on whom and how to pay out the inheritance when Jonathan and Sarah pass.

We stepped in to help drive down the rehab loan (which saved more than $50,000), and we stepped in to figure out what financial steps made the most sense. Since they have a substantial portfolio, by documenting the intra-family loan, the family keeps the inheritance distribution equitable among all seven children. Every family needs traffic cops to step in when it seems like the lights are out and everybody is driving in different directions.

Guardian Angel. One of my clients was a gentleman who worked for a small Philadelphia company. He made in the mid–five figures—a modest income but one that provided for his family. Well guess what? He was a winner in a multi-million-dollar lottery drawing, making millions for himself and his family. Wow! Talk about a life change. And he and his wife had the natural reaction: Let's redo the bathrooms in our home! Let's get a Mercedes! Let's buy a beach house! Buy! Buy! Buy! I get the sentiment. I really do.

But we've all heard the stories about the lottery winners who wind up bankrupt. Their eyes and desires are bigger than their wallets. The urge to splurge now is also often overwhelming to inheritors and successful athletes in particular. We didn't want to tell this couple that they couldn't buy things they once could not afford and would indeed make their lives more comfortable. But we also didn't want them to make the mistakes that plague so many. So here's what we came up with: we asked them to hit a six-month plus pause button—no spending on major purchases for the first six months. That would give them time to let their winning sink in, to evaluate what they really wanted, to tell those nearby with their hands out for a loan or gift that the window is closed. They could then see the extraordinary amount that later goes to Uncle Sam in taxes, and to put a bundle into investments to get a glimpse of how money can grow. Finally they would then be in a position to make the best decisions not only for their shorter-term wishes, but also for their long-term health. That, to me, was a huge victory—and one I'm very proud of, because we helped them protect themselves from, well, themselves.

A good fiduciary gives you the framework to make good decisions that are most beneficial to your current life and long-term goals, especially if you're dealing with the lack of experience, confusion, and complexities of life.

Puzzle Solver. You've got a lot of pieces to your life. Some may interconnect easily, and others may feel like they never fit. No matter the case, life is complex—and we're here to help fit the pieces in the best way possible.

Here's one of my favorite stories: Sally and Hank both had very comfortable careers (she in accounting, he in sales). They lived in a rural area of Pennsylvania and really wanted to stay there when they retired and be close to their families. They also wanted to help their kids with owning their own homes. So what ended up happening? They bought a large piece of property and divided off one or two acres for each of their children's families to have their own home on the bigger family farm.

We helped them achieve their main focus—family togetherness. Their long-term objective was for their offspring to enjoy the family compound together, long after they had both passed on. We supported their goal by looking at all of the financial pieces, the tax implications, and other logistical questions—and figured out how to get it done. But what makes me happiest is what their life has become. Sally and Hank host dinner for the extended family once a week, and the grandchildren come to their home to practice piano and take piano lessons every week. (And they even have enough money left over to fund a family vacation once a year with 20 to 30 people.) So Sally and Hank get what they want—not just money-wise, but also familywise. That is the joy we want to help facilitate, and if we can help you remove the obstacles and coordinate the moving pieces in life, that's perhaps the greatest role we can serve.

Roomba. It's not just because we can help clean up messes. But you know how a Roomba hits a wall and then just goes to a different location to suck up the crumbs? We do that too. Hit a wall? We can move in a different direction. A good fiduciary can change directions fast. As your goals or life situations change, we need to be able to adapt quickly, perhaps mobilize assets, and reevaluate targets. Our ability to move in changing directions is one of our strengths.

Career Changer. Jeanette was a successful senior executive in her family's business. She and her husband, Ron, made about $1 million a year. But she hated her job—mainly because she couldn't get along with her cousin, who was also a company executive. Ron was unhappy in his sales position, and he wanted more autonomy and felt stuck in his career. This is a common theme we see, of course, as people feel like they have no way out of bad situations because they fear not being able to make the money that they're currently making.

How did we help? We came up with an exit plan, and then we followed through: we searched for opportunities that would be the right fit at similar income levels. We found a company she could invest in and where she could become president. And we helped her transition financially into her new role. But that's not really the most important piece. The bigger point is that we held strategy sessions with her. By helping her identify her joys and pains, we could think through how she could make a change. Those tactics (and knowing someone has your back) are benefits you really can't put a price tag on.

I'm also happy to report that Jeanette's relationship is also better with her cousin now that she left the company. Maybe call us Family Healer too?

Train Station. We serve as the hub through which all decisions can travel. That's incredibly important in any kind of financial situation, especially complex ones. Example: just recently we talked to a couple whose daughter wanted to buy a multi-million-dollar apartment in California. She and her partner had been renting for so long (at close to $10,000 a month), and they felt like they were throwing their money away. They wanted to invest in a property. Only problem? She couldn't afford the price tag. In most cases advisers would say "no way" and move on. But because we have knowledge of the overall family dynamic—how much the elder couple has, how much the apartment means to the daughter, the tax implications, and more—we could offer solutions as long as we knew they wouldn't hurt my clients' income, estate, or tax situation. So we figured out an intra-family asset-protection trust loan, which had lower rate tax implications and better estate planning outcomes than a bank loan. This approach helped the couple fund a portion of their daughter's apartment. The daughter still has skin in the game. What's that worth? It's a heck of a lot more than you'd get from your big-box financial adviser who has thousands of clients.

Family Historian. Think about what happens if a fiduciary firm works with a family for years, even decades. We get to know them really, really well. We know their goals, their desires, their *life*. We also get to know their families. When the patriarch and/or matriarch passes, we can stay as the constant—helping the next generation not only with the logistics, but also with the emotional connections with the parents. We know and understand their values, mission, and desires in life. That, as we all know, is an important piece of who we are. While I'm certainly not suggesting that we're a part of the family (though I have had many a holiday dinner with clients who have become close friends), we can help be a sounding board and play an important role for generations to come.

Marriage Counselor. Most of us probably know that the number one thing couples fight about isn't sex or who unloads the dishwasher 97.3 percent of the time. It's money. We fight about spending too much, saving too little, and everything in between. Couples also fight because they don't even like talking about it, because they may be conflict averse, for example. How do we step in? We encourage differences of perspective, even conflicts at times, to come out; we talk them through, we help couples align values and/or learn to compromise, and we offer solutions for fixing what seems unfixable. In many ways, it's about communication, but it's also about having a third party involved—someone who's unbiased and not emotionally attached—to help couples see things more clearly and get on the same page. It's not about counseling per se, of course, but it does serve the role of conflict resolution.

Parent. Your parents told you "No" when you wanted to eat crayons for dinner. Now that you're an adult, few people have the authority to tell you "No" (cops and bosses are notable exceptions of course). And while one of our codes is that clients always have the final decision, fiduciaries will be honest with you when it comes to keeping your best interest in mind. So you can expect to hear "No" or "There is a better way" at some point in your journey. And just like with a parent, it's always done with your best interest at heart.

Teacher. I have a referral named Zo, who is a scientist born in another country, where his wife still owns thousands of acres of farmland. Nearing retirement, Zo came to us on the advice of a close, lifetime friend. We met, and we talked a lot about his priorities—his spirituality and his relationships with his family members being on the top of the list. He wanted some help with thinking about his finances and knowing how to reinvent and rethink his entire spending formula for the next 20 to 30 years. Included in our mission, he wanted to know how much he could spend in retirement. He wanted to know when he could retire, if he should pay off his mortgages, how much he could spend on traveling, kids' weddings, and issues like that. "That's your job," he told me. I said, "Yes, it is." And we helped him figure all those challenges out.

That's the obvious part of our job. We will help you figure out the complexity of your own financial puzzle. But here's where it gets interesting. Zo and his wife have four grown children, and he wanted to help them with their mortgages and help them learn about finances so they'd have the knowledge and skill sets that would serve them throughout life.

You know what I did? I linked the children up with two of our Certified Financial Planners who are also millennials so they could all be speaking the same language from the same generation. And I gave the children some reading assignments, which they would then use to jumpstart discussions with our advisers. The goal: we would help teach Zo's children about finance and their futures.

We don't want our clients in the dark when they make decisions. Quite the opposite actually. Education is one of our main missions because that's ultimately what is best for you and your family in the long run.

We involve families' children in all our processes (to the extent that you agree is best for everyone) to help teach them how to get started or progress on many critical issues involving finances and developing systematic wealth creation techniques. This can be a major service, as many of our clients are worried about how their kids will handle their wealth once they inherit. Teaching them about good financial habits early goes a long way to protecting a family's wealth since time is our most important asset (this issue is well covered in *Reinvent Rich* as one of the essential concepts of life).

Life Coach/Personal Trainer. How do you, as you approach retirement, expand your physicality—meaning your physical well-being and your mental well-being? They both have a role in how you approach other things in your life. We do strongly advocate for a healthy approach to life to help inform your purpose and your goals. Some examples include doing things to keep yourself physically active, mentally sharp, and emotionally joyful. When all of these things are aligned, it allows you to focus on the things you care about and helps you create even more freedom in your future life.

No, of course, we're not trying to be in the business of providing medical advice or showing you the correct running form to avoid shin splints. But we will ask you how to get beyond the "money" question. As a fiduciary firm, we help our clients by asking them to present us with a clearly articulated vision of their future, including what will give them significance and impact in their lives. This concept is based on one of Simon Sinek's books, *Start with Why*, which deals with issues of why we do what we do and how those actions are important to our future.

Legacy Keeper. Imagine a couple living a modest life in Idaho. They have two sons—one just getting by with no savings, the other starting out his career in the gig economy (lots of different jobs pieced together). Susan and Randall came into a lot of money (due to a family inheritance) recently, but they do not live an entitled life or have an entitled mentality. When they collected a significant inheritance (in the $9 million range), they were stressed. Their life went from vanilla to triple-scoop chocolate fudge delight just like *that*. How do you figure out estate taxes? How much cash do they need to supplement their modestly lived lives into their 60s and beyond? How much should they give to help their sons? (In addition, they're also scheduled to receive another large sum in the future from trust funds.)

We, of course, walked them through all of those questions with possible alternative solutions, but one of the greatest things we did was to get the sons involved (with their parents' approval of course). Though the sons had no experience with money and asset management, they were hard workers and they wanted to learn. We included them in separate individual conversations, we taught them about what we do, and we figured out the best ways to help them think about their newfound assets.

This approach, we suspect, will be the key for helping the sons make smart decisions when they in turn inherit the family fortune down the line. We hold meetings every 90 days, and that relationship-building schedule, I find, is what will be key to helping them reach their goals.

This really is the bottom line when it comes to a fiduciary's roles. Yes, we wear a lot of hats. But our mission is to make a major change: to move away from the transactional relationships that are so prevalent in the investment industry. Instead we want those relationships to be transformational.

From transactional to transformational…that's a pretty lofty goal, but one I strive to achieve every day of my career because ultimately that's what serves you.

Chapter 4

THE DECISION THAT MAKES A DIFFERENCE

**Compared to the big corporate product creators,
a nimble and experienced fiduciary firm will provide
the services and team that can help you come out
on top of accomplishing your missions in life.**

Imagine you bust something in your home—it's not major enough to call in a contractor, and you certainly think you could handle the task. You know what you need? Some glue! Yes, glue will get that broken keepsake back together.

Now you have a couple of choices. You could order some glue online. You could go to a big-box, sell-everything store. You could go to the neighborhood hardware store.

In the first case, you do a search, pick out one that looks good, maybe gets decent reviews, and has some packaging you like. Order it—boom, it's delivered right to your door.

In the second case, you go to the store that has it all, ask a sales associate for the glue aisle, find it, then pick the one with the best marketing lingo and perhaps the best price. And, oh, by the way, on the way out, you stop and end up buying 12 other things you didn't need, but what the heck, why not stock up on your 27th roll of duct tape while you're there? So you get the glue and end up spending way more than you had intended.

In the final scenario, you go to the neighborhood store, they greet you by name, and you ask about glue. Instead of pointing you to the aisle, they ask what your project is. You tell them that, holy moly, you can't believe that you broke your spouse's all-state swimming trophy. And they not only tell you which glue is best for the job, but they also walk you through tricks and instructions for how to do the best job possible—to make the task just a little bit easier and the outcome a whole lot better.

Do scenarios one and two have some advantages? Sure.

But I ask you, in the end, which experience and result are really, really the best? It's the third choice, no doubt—because it was about more than a purchase and more about customizing the advice to you and what *you* needed.

Surely you know I'm really not talking about a broken trophy, but about the kind of experience you get with smaller, family-oriented fiduciaries.

While there are a million options for wealth advisers, with some big-name firms, you simply can't match the experience and results you get with a personalized touch and a well-coordinated team.

Certainly my intention is not to bash other firms and what they offer, but I do think that to understand what smaller fiduciary firms do well, you have to understand how the big wealth advisers operate—and the caveats that go with them. Once you have a clear picture, then you can better make a decision about who to trust with your money, your family and life's challenges.

We'll spend this chapter looking at the differences and helping you navigate what can be a tricky world. After all, you may not have any knowledge (or interest in learning) about all the financial and logistical hurdles you'll face in life, so it's easy to be caught up in a tornado of mumbo jumbo and jargon that can sell you on a certain service.

Here are the ways:

Big firms want big producers, so they have big numbers. Here's the thing. It's a quality versus quantity issue. Think of the difference between eating in a mess hall or an intimate Italian restaurant. In the former you may well get the watery, instant mashed potatoes whether you want them or not. In the latter you can talk to the chef, tell her you like olive oil more than butter, really love parsley, and while you're at it, please throw in some fresh tomatoes too! Family-oriented firms throw in the tomatoes—and whatever else you want.

Big financial firms want their advisers to have lots and lots of clients (for reasons you'll see in a moment). So if an adviser manages a thousand or so portfolios, do you think you're going to get the personalized service that we offer? Do you think you can call up and explain a particularly complex situation you're having? Do you think the relationship is anything more than transactional? Likely not. Big firms churn through people. There's just not any other way when you oversee that many people and portfolios for a single adviser. Remember, they get incentivized with bonuses, so it's better when they can be juggling a thousand clients themselves. And you think you're going to get much phone or face time with your advisor? Not a chance that it's very often, and certainly not as often as we meet with our clients.

Big firms push products—and you pay for them. When you work with a fiduciary, we take pledges that the client comes first, above all other interests. Fiduciaries don't create and sell financial-investment products because that means that they'd be putting their interests (their financial success) in front of yours. But the big firms that aren't fiduciaries make boats—no yachts—of money on their products, such as internally created funds or similar investments. And then not only do they get percentages built into those products, but anytime other employees have their clients buy into the funds, they often get a piece of it. The fees may be so small that individual clients may not think much of it in the larger context of the portfolio, but that's how they're making oodles and oodles of money, through the fees that come from their very own products (even money-market funds), so you'll often be advised to invest in those products.

For example let's say Big Bad Brothers sells a real estate fund. Sounds like it's a good, solid, reliable fund. After all, it's with a reputable company. The advisers there will offer you their products and perhaps outside products to invest in, and they may well get commissions and fees based on them. A big deal? Maybe not that big. But isn't the bigger picture worth thinking about? What if another fund could get you more growth and income, but it's not recommended to you because their fee and commission are smaller? That happens all the time.

Sound like a conflict of interest to you? It sure does to me. A good firm should not be a product creator.

And that's not even mentioning the fact that these firms are frequently charging you twice: they're charging you for the products, and they're charging you a service fee to be your advisers. Now I like double-dipping when it comes to scoops of frozen yogurt, but I don't like it in this case. Who wins here? Not the client. They do. You earn less. They make more.

In bigger firms, there's more of a chance to have bad apples. Look, we have a small firm, and I intimately know how well every person performs, what each one does, how each one treats clients, and frankly whether any funny business is going on. In some fields it's no big deal if someone makes a mistake (ok, so they served you the rib eye instead of the porterhouse, you can ask for them to redo the order), but what happens when the mistake happens with your life savings or your estate? More is at stake. A lot more.

Firms that aren't fiduciaries lack objectivity. By design, if a firm does not serve as a fiduciary, its advisers may or may not be objective. They can say they try to put clients first, or they're committed to putting clients first, but they don't have an ethical obligation to do so without fiduciary initiatives in place. You deserve more. You deserve objectivity when it comes to your money, your family, and your future estate. Period.

Here is another good example of how it works in practice. A big firm will have an analyst who watches various funds. The big firm will typically rely on the recommendation of that analyst—i.e., should you buy, sell, or stay firm with General Motors stock right now? One analyst makes one prediction, and so there is influence within the ranks of advisers in buying or selling. Instead, isn't it better to look at what thirty firms' analysts are recommending for a certain stock to see the whole picture? I mean I get that a big firm has to trust its own analysts, but their judgment may be clouded if their firm has a direct business relationship with the company. You should wonder if their interests come before yours. Obviously, your potential financial benefit could be in jeopardy. We all want objectivity in decision making. Without it, don't you think you could be missing the boat?

Big financial firms don't help holistically. Having a professional network is the subject of my next chapter, so I won't go in too much depth here, but I'll leave it like this: we will help you with any problem big or small as it has an effect on your life. You think you can call up your investment adviser and ask him to negotiate a car price? Will he? Don't think so. We do it on an ongoing basis.

Fiduciaries are more than a service. We're advocates. We are here not only to advise you on financial matters, but also to serve as your advocate and be in your corner so you stay on track in life and coordinate our activities toward your goals. After all, with technology changing with increasing momentum, there's so much confusion in today's world. We can help you figure it out and thereby leverage your time.

Big firms typically don't think about generations. As I mentioned earlier, one of the things we do is educate entire extended families about critical financial issues. This is crucial to the long-term health of families, as people must learn about best practices, how to grow their assets, and how to protect their wealth. We teach, we interact, and we have multigenerational clients because our clients care not only about their own wallets, but also about the security and bigger futures of their younger family members once they're gone.

Being a fiduciary means you build relationships. Being a fiduciary is all about creating a relationship with a family that changes the focus from transactional to transformational. You get that with personal commitments from multiple team members. You get that with relationships. You don't get that when you're on hold for 34 minutes and some adviser—who may be changing frequently—recommends the fund that fits in some model and may or may not be better for the firm.

But I come from a place where I think you deserve more—and that's where fiduciaries come in. We help you get what you want—not just from a dollars and cents point of view, but from a holistic, family view that life is complicated, and you can use someone in your corner to help you fight your fight to get what you want out of life.

Product Creators Versus Family-Focused Fiduciaries

An at-a-glance guide showcasing the differences between the two

Family-Focused Fiduciaries	Product Creators*
A team that is dedicated to helping a small number of clients to receive personalized attention, service, and advice	One adviser with a few assistants who oversees hundreds, maybe thousands, of clients
Takes a multigenerational approach, working with a family (or individual) consisting of as many branches on the family tree as are wanted	Often only deals with the "big" client
Has no financial interest in any services or products to give clients the best wealth advice in the best interest of the client, not the firm, and is compensated by the client	Creates and sells internally managed or organized products, like mutual funds or ETFs that are the cornerstone of what is offered to clients
Unbiased advice	Advice often clouded by the top-down directives for these products
Offers wide range of services and connects client to a wide variety of professionals to help not only increase wealth, but also free up time and lower stress	Often only deals with financial matters and investments
Listens more, talks less	Talks more, listens less
Client meetings as needed, and regular ones scheduled in time intervals based on the client needs	May only have occasional, more sporadic client meetings

* *Like big investment firms similar to wire houses or banks.*

How Many Fiduciaries Are There?

In 2021 there were over 263,000 total financial advisers, according to the Bureau of Labor Statistics. How many of them do you think are fiduciaries? About 6 percent. That's based on the number of advisers who are registered investment advisers (RIAs), who are required to be fiduciaries to stay registered with the SEC. Now there's no way of knowing how many of them are part of small, family-oriented firms, but you get the point: just because someone advises you on your money doesn't mean they accept the responsibilities as outlined by the Certified Financial Planner® Board's Fiduciary Standard.

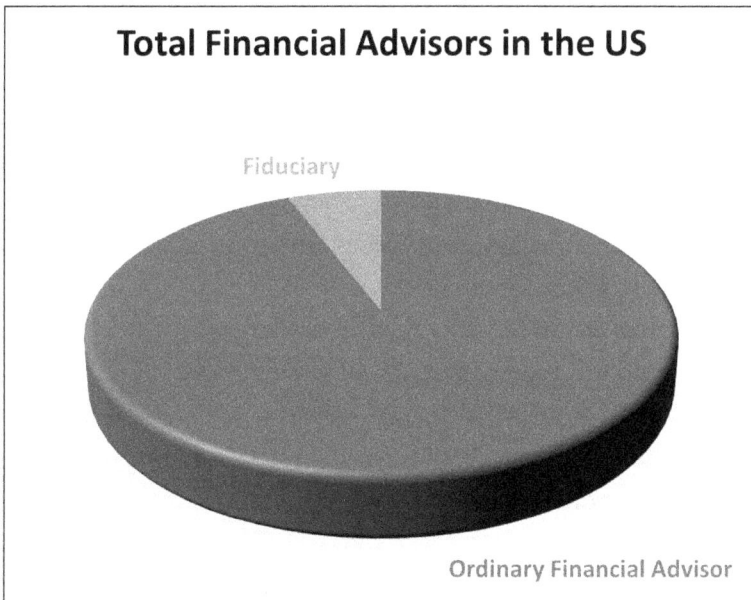

Total Financial Advisors in the US

Fiduciary

Ordinary Financial Advisor

Data Source: US Bureau of Labor Statistics, 2021

Chapter 5

WHO'S GOT YOUR BACK?

**Finding the right firm for you is all about
knowing the secret sauce for success.**

Finding a fiduciary isn't like finding a new restaurant to try. You don't
search Yelp, look at reviews, scan Instagram for mouth-watering photos
of taquitos, check out the menu, then make a reservation for four just
in time for your group to make the Mega-Margarita special. Nope, the
decision to find a fiduciary is much bigger than deciding where you'll
dip your chip. This decision influences every aspect of your life—and
the ramifications will last a lot longer than one little meal.

And let's be honest: a fiduciary is a term and concept that few people have really spent a lot of time looking at, so there really aren't many
comprehensive resources that will help you navigate this world, unlike
other ubiquitous services, like hotels, restaurants, doctors, and more.
And isn't that crazy? A fiduciary can have a huge impact on a variety of
major aspects of your life. And that makes navigating this world that
much tougher.

The choice for a fiduciary is a big one, but even narrowing down the list to begin with can feel daunting. So let's take a quick look at the best practices for finding a capable, committed fiduciary firm that will assist you in so many aspects of your financial and other areas of life. Here's the process I recommend:

Talk to friends. It's the most frequent way we get clients. People tell their friends, "You should talk to Irvin." So what happens is that a person or family shares their concerns or problems with a close friend, and that friend, who understands the depth of insights and capabilities available, recommends our firm. And that's how the conversation—and a potentially long relationship—begins.

There is a tricky element to all of this, though. After all, what's the one thing you've been conditioned to never talk about with people, even those close to you? (No, it's not politics—that notion is out the window with so many now sharing their political viewpoints 24/7 on social media.) It's money.

Don't talk about money or finances with anyone! That's how many of us have lived. Now I'm not suggesting you email your PINs to a friend or reveal your net wealth or give away any personal info, but I am suggesting that if you're having trouble or concerns or dilemmas you can't quite figure out how to solve, talk to a close person who may be able to relate. Give the general idea and simply start the conversation (and ideally do it with someone you would expect would use a fiduciary). You never know who knows who and how that person may be able to help. Or, of course, just straight out ask people in your network if they know of any fiduciaries and if they have any recommendations. Word of mouth works well to begin finding a fiduciary.

We had one prospect meeting a few years ago that was a referral from a longstanding client couple of ours who both work at a well-known pharmaceutical company. The prospect and her husband became paralyzed by the amount of wealth they accumulated through salary and inheritance. In our discovery meeting, we asked if they were looking at other advisers. They said no. "We trust our friend, so we trust you!" Five hours later we had a new client and learned volumes about them, from family stories to their kids' sports activities to where they go on vacation. (See Chapter 7 for what to expect from initial meetings.)

Do your background checks. Once you get the names of a few firms, it's smart to do background checks to make sure they don't have any complaints or lawsuits against them. (I'm proud to say that in 27+ years since the founding of our firm, we have a clean record on all team members.) For registered investment advisers with more than $115 million of client assets under management, they must be registered with the SEC. You can look up the adviser's track record with the SEC (adviserinfo.sec.gov) or with Brokercheck (brokercheck.finra.org). This additional government website can also be used to check out your investment professional (https://www.investor.gov/introduction-investing/getting-started/working-investment-professional/check-out-your-investment).

See who's a "public" expert. One of the ways you can get an inkling about how good a firm is would be to check to see if they have any public expertise. That is, do they write about matters of finances, wealth, and related areas? Do they have a book about the subject of fiduciaries? Now being public doesn't guarantee high quality, but it may give you a body of work to evaluate. That is, does what they say align with your own values and some of the qualities we've gone over in this book? Can you get a sense of what they do, who they serve, problems they solve, and areas of expertise through what they write or talk about?

Ask the questions. Once you identify a handful of firms that you'd like to look into, you can set up meetings. They'll likely want to ask you a lot of questions (see Chapter 7), but you should feel empowered to reverse the roles and ask a lot of questions too—some of which can be formed by what you've learned in this book. How would you approach the X problem I'm having? What's your main investment strategy? Who is in your professional network that will be able to help me? Speaking of which, let's go to that very subject—and why it's one of the most important roles that a capable fiduciary can play.

Play the long game. When you're talking to folks, try to get a sense of what the firm is interested in. Certainly they are in the business of making money for their firm, so they should be up front about their fee structure. They should not be pressuring you to make decisions fast, to sign on the dotted line before you leave the office, or anything like that. They should want your discussions to lead to a long-term relationship. Firms that put extra pressure on you to make fast decisions may fall into the red-flag category in how they view your potential relationship. You will get a sense of their priorities when you meet with them and begin discussions.

I hope this perspective gives you a logical start as you look for a firm that can serve your needs. Of course my team and I are happy to meet with you as well as give insight into who we are, what we do, and how we can help with your search. (We serve a national footprint of clients and serve many families who aren't local to our region.) We can answer any questions you might have about what to look for and how to find someone who is best suited for you and your family.

But the big point here is to be patient and really use your own network of people to see if you can get some inside information on people and firms you can trust. As we all know, personal recommendations hold much more weight than the Almighty Google can ever provide.

The Health Benefit of Using a Fiduciary

We all know and appreciate the benefits of managing stress in your life—stress reduction has a positive influence on decreasing risks of heart disease and more. It's no secret that financial stress ranks as one of the top triggers in life, so you can easily see that if you can find ways to help manage your financial fears and stresses, it will have long-term benefits in life! I should also say very clearly that there's really no such thing as totally *eliminating* stress. Stress (and the accompanying notion of problem solving) is part of the price of living. That said, our role is to reduce a whole heck of a lot of it!

Chapter 6

TEAMWORK MAKES THE DREAM WORK

The right fiduciary will provide access to a capable and trusted professional network of people who will help every step of the way.

In a lot of ways, I see myself as an air traffic controller. Your life has one plane coming in, one plane leaving, a lot of planes on the tarmac waiting to take off, weather delays, and a 6-month-old baby who's wailing so loud that your ears feel like they're in the front row of an AC/DC concert. Life is a *lot*. And our job is to partner with you in your comings and goings smartly and safely so you can kick back, relax, and enjoy this flight we call life.

After all, your whole life can revolve around stresses—the stress of a job, the stress of family situations, the stress of money issues, and the stress of the daily grind. And while I'd be naive if I said I could remove all of your stresses, I can confidently say that my work as a fiduciary is to, one, help reduce them and, two, give you back time to do more of what you want and less of what you don't want. A lot less.

When you look at the growing inflation that we're all coping with, the chart below depicts a dire outlook about inflation and money. You need all the support you can get from a fiduciary to help you deal with life and your stress.

MONEY, INFLATION A SOURCE OF STRESS FOR MANY U.S. ADULTS

AMERICAN PSYCHOLOGICAL ASSOCIATION

Inflation is a source of stress for 83% of U.S. adults

56% of all adults, during the prior month, have had to make different choices due to a lack of money

% OF ADULTS WHO INDICATED MONEY WAS A SIGNIFICANT SOURCE OF STRESS

57% said that having enough money to pay for things in the present (like rent/mortgage) is their main source of financial stress

43% reported feeling that saving enough money for things in the future is their main source of stress

Latino/a adults
66%

Black adults
59%

White adults
52%

Asian adults
45%

STRESS IN AMERICA™ 2022

© 2022 American Psychological Association

As you can see from the chart above, stress makes people even more nervous about utilizing their resources. We provide leverage for you as we give you your time back to devote to more of the other more important things in your life.

Here is one clear fact: many people are confused—confused about Covid, confused about our government's leadership, confused about foreign conflicts or inflation, confused about investments, or confused about day-to-day decisions that come at them like darts. Here's the main way we reduce the confusion about coping with day-to-day dilemmas:

I have built a professional network that my clients have access to, so they can get life-changing questions answered. After all, as a fiduciary, I don't claim to know everything about everything (how could anyone?). But our team can put our clients in touch with the people who do know. That's our goal: if you're stuck in the minutiae of life, we can get you unstuck by getting you the solutions you need. No question is too odd, no situation is too formidable, no uh-oh is oh-no. We say, "Oh yes," because we know that we can likely connect you with people in our network (which is always expanding, by the way) who can help.

The value of this network is a theme you will see over and over in this book: stop spending time and headaches on things out of your area of expertise, because when you let our team and our network help you, you get back more time to do what you love with the people you care most about.

And to put a fine point on this: this connection we make for our clients may very well be one of the most important things we do for them while we help them create and protect their wealth. We give them access to the people they need—and the people it might take hours upon hours to find themselves. That network and efficiency can be priceless for people with major questions or confusion—and with little time to figure it out themselves.

In Chapter 3, you saw the long list of types of things we do—from managing your money to negotiating deals to helping solve family conflicts. In addition I feel like one of our main roles is as a connector—making sure you get what you need from the people you need. I tend to think of our network in three main categories:

The Basics. Everyone—dealing with estates, finances, and complex financial hurdles or situations—needs certain people. Those people or firms generally fall into the categories of accountants and attorneys, actuaries, or trust experts. Settlement companies and other real estate professionals handle home and real estate–related matters (real estate tends to be one of the major alternative client investments and a good way to use and protect assets and minimize taxes). These firms handle many of the basic and advanced moving parts of the challenges you have, and we will work with them to make sure the whole team is unified in its approach. That's one of our primary values—connecting all the disparate parts so that they're moving together to the desired outcome. Consider your fiduciary the hub on a wheel through which all different spokes travel.

The Specializations. You remember the story I told about the couple who sold their artwork? We worked with two major auction houses to get it done. That doesn't happen by googling "auction houses" and cold calling. That happens because we have a longstanding relationship with the experts there, so we can explain the opportunity to get the deal done. Situations may be different, but our network consists of people who can help with various assets, whether it be cars, art, antiques, company sales or purchases, or whatever major assets you have. Amazingly we also have subcategories of people in all these areas—specific car experts for domestic/imported car acquisitions and others for exotic or specialty ones. In fact, several of the firms in our network are some of the country's most renowned experts in car collecting and fine arts. Think that comes in handy if people are looking to assess the value of some of their art, antiques, or collectible assets? Rather than them wondering, "I wonder how much my X, Y, or Z is worth, and I wonder how to find someone to tell me the truth," they can come to us and—because we've developed long relationships built on trust—we can deliver the expert who will give them the scoop with very little fuss or friction. It's hard to put a price on that kind of access to a network of life specialists.

The "Are You Kidding Me?" Category. Look, I meant it when I said that no problem was too crazy to ask. On the local level, we have architects, electricians, and tree arborists in our network because I've tried to help clients solve nagging problems with their homes. Remember, we don't want you spending time doing the drudgery. Seriously, I remember one client was telling me how his toilet kept backing up at his shore house, and it was driving him crazy. We referred him a highly skilled local plumber he needed (because he had a good reputation and I had worked with him extensively through other clients previously). We also have a traveling pastor in our network. I met him at a client's funeral in which he did a marvelous job of telling the life story of a dear friend and client. I thought, *Wow, you never know when one of our clients may need someone like him for some issue in their life*, so I invited him to get involved as a mentor within our network.

You tell us your problem, and our team will reach out to find a qualified resource who can address it. We don't want you to waste your time on Google, or worse, let a problem fester because it's too daunting to tackle.

To get a better sense of the big picture, look at this partial snapshot of our

Network List of Specialist Firms:

Financial Professionals	Personal Services Specialists	Specialists for the Home
CFO/Consultant	Decorative Arts Antiques	Interior Designer
Estate Attorney	Consultant	Plumbing/Heating/AC
CPA/Accountant/Tax Preparer	Fine Arts/Antiques Auction	Real Estate Evaluation and Sales
Real Estate Tax Specialist	House Services	Architect
TPA/Retirement Planning	Jewelry/Antique Jewelry	Home Cleaning
Specialist	Auction House	Electrician
Commercial Building Cost	Independent Automotive	Landscaper
Segregation Specialist	Specialists (New and	Contractor
Nonprofit Consulting Attorneys	Preowned)	Tree Arborist
Real Estate Settlement Title	Domestic, Imported, and	Moving Services
Agency	Collectible Cars	Sound and Audio Specialist
Personal Insurance Services		Window Cleaning
Independent Life Insurance and		Custom Exterior Lighting
Creative Trust Services		Specialist
Tax Planning Services/Trusts		Lawn Sprinkler Specialist
Asset Protector Independent		
Trust Company		
Title Insurance/Settlement		
Specialist		
Monthly Bill Paying and		
Tracking Specialist (in person		
or virtual)		
Entrepreneurial Coaching		

Personal Growth	Healthcare Services	Work
Pastor/Mentor/Grief Consultant	Home Mobility Services	IT Specialist
Continuing Care Retirement	Consumer Empowerment,	Commercial Cleaning Services
Community Evaluations and	Medicare, SSI Insurance	
Transition Management	Analysis	
Longevity Consulting Services	Health and Longevity	
	Consultants	

That's a lot of different kinds of resources we can connect you with. We are always looking for new firms to add to our network because ultimately there are always new problems to solve.

In any case you get the point: your fiduciary's job is to make your life easier. The way to do it is with a village, and you want to make sure that your fiduciary has an excellent one.

Chapter 7

SHALL WE DANCE?

What to expect from your initial meetings—and what you should do to prepare.

OK, this is going way-way-way-waaaaaaaaay back for me, but I think we all remember what first dates are like. They can be fun, they can be awkward (especially when a massive peppercorn snuggles into your front teeth), they can be a tap dance of conversation—each person talking, listening, laughing, and feeling out whether it's worth a second date.

That can be the way a lot of professional relationships start (minus the fettuccine alfredo). There are conversations, there are questions, there are tangos where both parties try to figure out if the fit is right.

That's no different when it comes to finding a fiduciary. You will have initial meetings and conversations to discuss services offered, goals, fee structures, and more. That's all to say there's not a "one and only way" to do things. The important thing is you must figure out what is right for you.

Here's what to expect from initial conversations. That plural form of the word conversation is vital here; you don't have to expect to make a decision after one talk. This isn't a sales pitch for a timeshare in Aruba. This is really a courtship in which we try to figure out whether we'll make that Ideal Partnership. Some guideposts:

Ask a lot of questions. You should feel like you're there to gather a lot of information about many of the topics we cover in this book. Ask about their services, their professional network, their accessibility, success stories, common mistakes people make, and issues important to you. You'll get a sense of their history and how they work, which will help you see if they are a good fit.

Expect to answer a lot. Good fiduciaries won't be selling themselves to you. They'll be asking you about you. They'll want to know your goals, your dreams, your pain points, and much more. Fiduciaries work best as your advocate when they know what makes you tick, what problems you've had, and where you want to go. So in many ways a good fiduciary is like a good doctor trying to figure out a medical mystery in order to put all the pieces together and come up with optimal solutions for you and your family. We have to know, ultimately, what's important to you and what the hurdles are for you living the life you want. To that end you can expect a perceptive fiduciary to ask you all sorts of questions—some of which may feel like they have nothing at all to do with a 401K, IRA, or mutual fund. Some of the questions we ask in the initial meetings:

- What are your personal and professional goals?
- What's important about money to you?
- What does a successful life look like when you're 45, 55, 65, 75, 85?
- What is your vision to create wealth for your family?

- What are your quality-of-life desires?
- How do you save and invest?
- How do you earn your money?
- What were your best and worst experiences with a professional adviser?
- If you didn't have to work anymore, what would you do?
- What relationships are most important to you?
- How does your family fit into your future financial goals?

And that's just a fraction of what we ask. You can see how this takes more than just a simple conversation. Our discovery meetings usually span the course of multiple meetings in this initial stage. We place more value on the process that happens even after the initial talks. This is about relationship building. The more we know about your interests and goals, the better we can serve you and be your advocate. In reality it takes us about a year to two years to really get to know the client (but I say that as a way of explaining that this is a learning process and a long-term relationship, not a boom-boom-boom transaction).

Discuss fee structure. For a fiduciary firm this discussion should be open book and transparent. With a fiduciary firm you won't see any fees charged on stock, bonds, or products, as we've discussed. But you can price shop and compare costs to services received. The important point is, are you getting the services you want and deserve for the fee you're paying? Here we have several cost structures—one based on assets under management, one an annual consulting fee/retainer, or an hourly rate. We discuss all the options and the scope of engagement—the advantages and disadvantages to each. You should walk through the fee structures with every fiduciary you talk to and base your decision not only on the fee, but also on the services you get for those fees. In the end it's really not about the fee; it's about the services we can provide you in creating and protecting your wealth, giving you back your time, reducing your stress, and supporting you in solving your life problems—the services that have massive value and really don't have price tags.

Know what you're getting into before you commit. While these early meetings can be a feeling-out process, you should have at least made an important step in your own mind: Are you ready to commit to working with a team? I remember one prospect—a married couple who were doctors living in Pennsylvania and owned their medical practice in New Jersey. They had about $10 million in publicly traded assets held at a large, well known mutual fund company and were do-it-yourself investors. They were referred to us because they wanted guidance on how to manage their assets upon selling their practice, so we had a meeting with them before they sold their practice in 2019. Later they determined they were comfortable continuing to manage their finances on their own and merely needed to evaluate the sale of their practice. Oftentimes it can be a struggle for do it yourself (DIY) investors to evaluate the value of a fiduciary financial adviser. It's not all just about selecting investments and creating asset allocations. It's the cash flow planning, tax planning, estate planning, outside professional network guidance and connections, and life coaching that a fiduciary can bring to your table. So it's helpful to know which services you really need if you are a DIY investor.

Remember, trust is earned. Nobody expects you to divulge everything in a first meeting with someone. You should think about initial meetings as setting up a foundation for the first year. What are your top three priorities? What are your goals? What do you want to accomplish in the near and longer term?

Ultimately you have to think of these early meetings as a time for us to get to know each other. It can be difficult to disclose personal details that we're so used to keeping private, but the end goal is one that we all value and all share: we want what's best for you.

Chapter 8

DOES YOUR FINANCIAL FITNESS PASS THE TEST?

The money-making and money-saving strategies that will help you clean up your finances and make your money grow.

By now you've heard me talk about the most important things in your life (other than nailing down a Wordle in two tries): family, freedom, and time. Those are the essential priorities that fiduciaries can have a direct impact on—giving you time and freedom back to do the things you enjoy with the people you love.

But let's not ignore the elephant in the room: the cash and the creation of wealth.

The fact is that time and freedom come with the fruits of your labor. That is, money doesn't buy everything, no, but it sure does come in handy when your passion is treating your extended family to a two-week jaunt to the Swiss Alps or Hawaii, or weekends away together as a family.

The flip side of not having or making enough money, as we know, is spending too much of it when you have it. That is, just because you make a lot doesn't mean you can live life like queens and kings and spend, spend, spend. To get my point across, let's take a page out of my earlier book *Reinvent Rich* to help your teenage children become millionaires. The process starts with developing discipline in work and savings at an early age, and then have a chat about muffins. I like muffins, but it doesn't have to be a blueberry muffin for you like it is for me… insert your favorite breakfast pastry or Starbucks latte of choice. Spending $7 bucks or so a day might sound trivial to you, but in the end, it's costing you dearly. If they invested that $7 a day in a pre-tax retirement account averaging 8% annual returns, they'd be millionaires in their retirement years. Make your own muffins or coffee for pennies on the dollar and enjoy the fruits of your labor. Don't believe me… check out the muffin chart for yourself.

Now, I'm not trying to rap you over the head, but you need to be smart, make good choices, and do the things that provide you financial security and the flexibility you deserve. The metaphor remains the same though… DON'T fall prey to the muffin!

How Much is that Daily Muffin and Coffee Costing You?	
If you saved the $7+ each day, and invested it weekly at 8 percent, you would be able to accumulate the following amounts over the following periods:	
5 years:	$15,650
10 years:	$38,990
25 years:	$203,130
44 years:	$1,000,000

So while we provide our clients with simple tips like the muffin above, what we really do is much more complex. A good fiduciary can help you with all aspects of your finances.

We can help you make more money—through wise investing and asset allocation.

We can help you manage your finances—looking carefully at your spending habits and helping you make tough choices (do you really need five cars just because you like one for every season, plus an extra?).

We can help you work through family conflicts—the very situation where so many financial fights originate and fester.

With 30+ years of working with families, I have seen it all (and our experience is all about helping you avoid the mistakes we've seen being made). I have seen great successes, I have seen great challenges, and I have seen comebacks that are more dramatic than ones on ESPN documentaries.

While fiduciaries can do a lot of the tough work, the ultimate responsibility still starts and ends with the client. This chapter will serve as a review of my favorite financial tips and advice, as featured in my first book, *Reinvent Rich*. First, though, let's look at a few family situations to see what lessons their stories can provide.

One couple, Sally and Gary, came to us talking about their readiness to retire next year. Sally was near 60, and Gary was in his mid-60s. Sally had saved nothing, and Gary had a mid-six-figure balance in his retirement account. They wanted to know when they could retire. Our answer: you're stuck. Like many couples who don't get started saving early and get distracted by the wheel-turning of life, they woke up and thought, "What happened? We have virtually nothing to show for the life we're living." And they were panic stricken.

While we can help, the bottom line is that they would need to continue to work past the age they wanted to retire or reduce their lifestyle expenses because they hadn't started saving early enough—and now they wouldn't be able to enjoy the freedoms provided from living a hard-working life.

On the other hand, remember our client who started with about $120,000 and inherited about the same amount? He looks back with a big smile on his once modest goal, and his life in retirement is rich, full, and secure as he is now even paying for friends on trips with him in his solo life. He was able to catch up financially, but only because he really listened to our team and lived within his means.

Another family recently wrote me a note; I've worked with this couple for many, many years. Barb was a young widow with a small child and very modest funds. She trusted us to help her take care of her and her son, as she continued on with her life. She got remarried to a man named Sam and was able to save, save, and save. She wrote years later, in part, "All we can say is thank you for taking care of me and now us…Two South Philly kids, just high school graduates who lived within our means, saved while we worked, and trusted you, cannot believe we have hit our family's ultimate financial goal. We are overwhelmed and grateful."

Now it's crucial to say this: money is relative. One million dollars to Sam and Barb may not be the same as one million dollars to another couple. The amount you have—and can comfortably live on—depends on the lifestyle you want. The key is that the income (after paying Uncle Sam) has to match the lifestyle; if it doesn't, that's where we see more problems than a plumber without a wrench.

In any case—no matter how much you start with, how much you have, or how much you want to make—there are some common financial principles that everyone should follow to best maximize their estate and get all the benefits that come with being financially flush and secure. Here are the mandates:

Save Early, Save a Lot: It's the most obvious tip, but it's the most important, because it will be the number-one thing you can do to reduce financial stress. The more you save and the earlier you start saving, the more you will make—and the more freedom you will have. For me that means saving ten cents for every dollar you make for your future before you pay your expenses. That also means contributing the maximum pretax deductions from your earnings and taking full advantage of matching programs to really make your money grow. It's not always easy to see your future 20 or 30 years down the line, but the more you make this a priority, the better you will sleep at night.

In the graph on the next page Sally saves $10,000 per year starting at year 1, and Bob saves $10,000 per year starting at year 11. Their accounts are both pre-tax qualified accounts and no funds are withdrawn to pay taxes during the 40 years. A 7% average annual rate of return is used. The lesson here folks is quite simple. Sally started saving early and ended up with more than twice as much as Bob. Save early. Save often. Time is your friend.

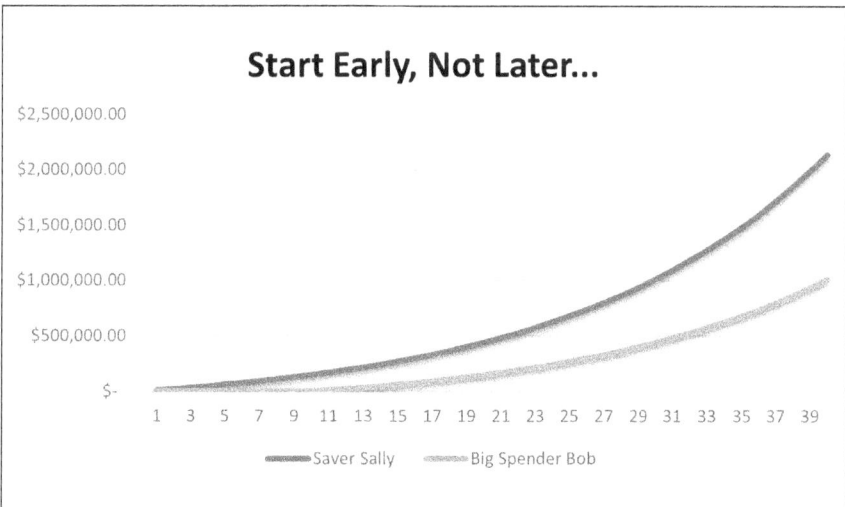

Start Early, Not Later...

Take Advantage of Dollar-Cost Averaging: The results can be as-tounding. The reason saving early and often is so important is because of the concept of dollar-cost averaging—meaning that your money grows exponentially. If you're 50 when you start saving, it's the accu-mulated value of pennies to what you'd have if you started saving when you were 20—because the total value compounds and compounds and compounds. It feels almost like free money, and it will take a huge burden off of you.

Make Your Budget Your Bible: Make financial decisions based on numbers, not emotion! The biggest problem I see with many fami-lies—wealthy or not wealthy—is that they spend way more than they make. So they get into debt, they don't save enough, they're always scrambling, and they're living the burden of an extremely stressful life. The couples who become true successes understand their income and understand that they need to make choices (no, you don't really need that Lamborghini or high-dollar dressage horse). Smart families com-municate their wants, look at the budgets, see where they can cut so they can afford the important things they want, and know that tough choices facilitate good ones later.

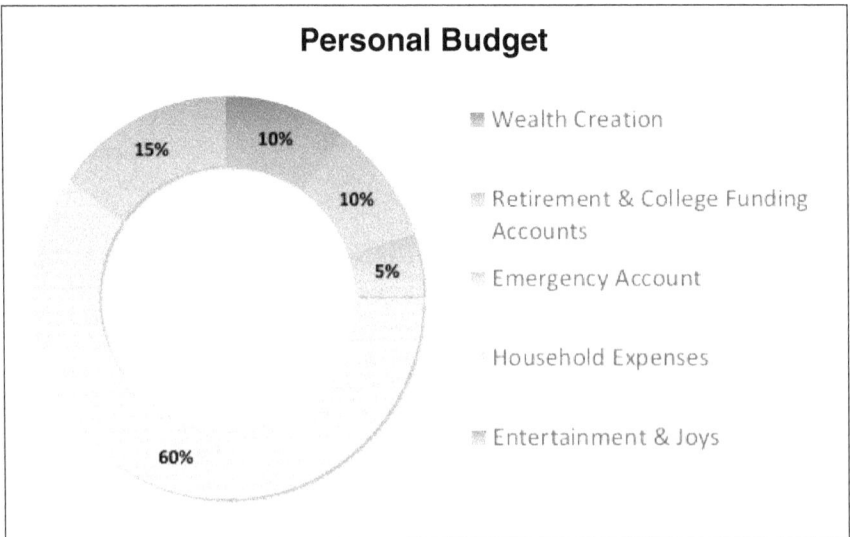

Personal Budget

- Wealth Creation — 10%
- Retirement & College Funding Accounts — 10%
- Emergency Account — 5%
- Household Expenses — 60%
- Entertainment & Joys — 15%

What a Typical Personal Budget Should Look Like

10% for wealth creation—to save and invest (before you pay your expenses)

10% for retirement and college-funding accounts

5% for an emergency liquidity account

60% for household expenses

15% for entertainment and joys

Explore Values along with Expenses: I always like to start our relationship with clients by telling them that the first thing we're doing isn't looking at the cable bill. The priority is that you—as an individual, a couple or as a family—need to articulate your family values. What's **important** to you? What makes you happy? What are your priorities? Do you like to travel, or do you value education more highly? Do you want experiences or things? When you have a shared vision, you can make better choices. And when you have competing visions, communicating about compromises, and sharing is the first step to make smart financial choices.

Gut Check

Part of the "gut check" process is about being honest with yourself and really diving deep into what you want, what worries you, and how you can manage it all. As a starting point to finding your favorite fiduciary, a fiduciary will ask some of these questions to help you get to the heart of it all. But you can also perform a self-check by asking yourself the following questions. It will help to write down the answers to prepare for your meeting with the team.

What are you saving for?
What do you like spending money on?
What worries you most about your finances?
Where is most of your debt?
What are your family's financial strengths?
What are your family's financial weaknesses?
Briefly define what wealth means to you.

High Risk = High Reward: When you're young, investing more assertively is often the better option because that's where you can experience more growth (not such a smart move as you get closer to retirement). But some people aren't comfortable with highly volatile investments, and they should look at more conservative approaches. In any case a diverse portfolio for your investments is your best strategy to take advantage of different ways to invest and to protect yourself when various asset classes or sectors underperform. This is certainly where we can come in to help you manage that diversity—and to determine your tolerance for risk over time (I call mine Irvin's Stomach Ulcer Index!).

Set Aside Time for You: Let me be clear with this: just because I strongly recommend saving and making tough decisions, that does not mean that you have to live like a hermit eating Spam and rice every day. Life is about living. And having fun. And doing cool things. And buying stuff that gives you joy. And seeing the world. And buying that beautiful dressage horse if that's what you love. The point is this: budget those things into your life. After all, the point of being financially savvy and secure isn't just about making sure you have enough money for retirement; it's also about making sure you have the funds for fun in life too.

Get on Track

If you feel like you need to hit the reset button when it comes to your financial picture, I'd suggest looking at the 21-Day Wealth Makeover in my book, *Reinvent Rich*. Does that mean you'll go from debt to diamonds in three weeks? Of course not. But my 21 day plan is all about getting started and laying down the foundation for good financial processes and habits.

Now I'll end this chapter with one of my favorite stories about money strategy, which is actually about a friend.

This couple—George and Phyllis—is not affluent, but not struggling. He does a lot of financial consulting on a part-time basis to augment his income but faced a tough road during Covid-19. He's in the middle of pivoting his career and in the business of buying medical practices. Their main investment strategy beyond their individual jobs is this: they bought homes in places where they like to vacation, such as New England, Florida, and Colorado. They took advantage of low interest rates and found properties that had motivated sellers. They also made sure to buy homes that were large enough to hold their own family. So they can spend their family vacations at one of the spots and then rent it out the rest of the year to others (and they take their vacation times off-peak season so they don't cut into the popular and more lucrative times of the year to rent the properties out).

With their kids grown, George and Phyllis can now use those properties for their own kids to enjoy for their family vacations, and they have enough properties that they can rotate and not feel like they're always going to the same place. During their child-rearing years, they paid down the principal on their mortgage loans and received valuable tax deductions to shelter their family income. Also they can use a 1031 exchange to defer gains on the eventual sale profits and reduce taxes paid to Uncle Sam.

Think about their financial advantage: they can generate income from the rentals (enough to pay the mortgage); they save money on their own vacations because they're not paying hotel or rental costs; they could make even more money if and when they're ready to sell properties, as real estate can be a tremendous income generator in the right market and at the right time. In fact it's a very smart retirement strategy if they want to sell one or more properties when they're ready to retire.

George and Phyllis are a good example of having a balanced portfolio with liquid and nonliquid assets in a diversified portfolio. (Note: where fiduciaries can come in is helping to negotiate borrowing rates, identify real estate agents to select well located properties, work through tax implications, and take care of many other financial and logistical details.)

Also take a look at the bigger picture. They not only created a smart financial strategy. They created opportunities to spend time with the people they love, doing what they enjoy and building the family unity they want as the whole family meets at the family properties at the "right time of year."

They created wealth. And they created something even more valuable.

Dollar-Cost Averaging Creates Compounded Wealth Over Time

Basically it's the technique in which you buy a fixed-dollar amount of a particular investment on a schedule, no matter the share price, no matter whether it's up or down (you simply buy more shares when it's low and fewer shares when it's high). Here's how it works:

Month	Stock Price	Dollars Invested	Shares Purchased
Month 1	$10.00	$500	50
Month 2	$9.40	$500	53.2
Month 3	$8.80	$500	56.8
Month 4	$9.30	$500	53.8
Month 5	$9.80	$500	51.0
Month 6	$10.50	$500	47.6
TOTAL		$3,000	312.4

After the six months at the current stock price, the total investment would be worth $3,280, which is a 9.3 percent gain on the $3,000 that was invested. But the stock has only gained 5 percent ($10.50 from $10). This is the beauty of dollar-cost averaging; by making regular purchases and buying stocks both when they are high as well as when they are low, in many cases you can lower your overall costs of investment relative to buying at a given point in time. Also, dollar-cost averaging takes much of the emotion out of investing, as it requires regular, systematic purchases. For those reasons I highly recommend this as a strategy for adding to the investments you already have.

Chapter 9

MAKE IT LAST

What a long-term relationship with a fiduciary should look like—and what you can do to make sure it's an effective team effort.

In life some relationships seem like they last only a minute (your high school crush?). Some last a little longer (it's a special thing when your barista learns your name and your usual order). Some we expect to be only temporary (yes, Doc, it's time for my colonoscopy), and some we expect to last a lifetime (your family).

Well if all goes well, your relationship with your fiduciary could and should last not only your lifetime, but also beyond that—including generations to follow. That's how vital a strong fiduciary can be to family success and happiness.

What makes it so? Well, first and foremost it stems from the benefits you receive, all of which I have outlined up to this point. Secondly it's because this relationship could well expand and grow to include future generations. How does that look in practice, and how do you ensure the relationship grows into an excellent one? My take for the elements that should be in place, and what you and a fiduciary should do to make it a long-lasting bond, is as follows.

Expect regular check-ins. We typically meet with our clients every 90 days at a minimum (and more or less than that if they prefer; we meet with some folks monthly and some yearly). But we find that every 90 days is just about the perfect time for Zoom or in-person meetings so that we can discuss finances or whatever else is on your mind (or check in on any life changes).

Expect personal touches. When we meet four times a year, suffice it to say we get to know you. Not just the numbers in your bank account, but so many other things—the name of your dog or cat, the health of your aunt, your preference of sports teams, what your kids are considering for their careers, the secret ingredient in that meatloaf casserole, you name it. That has nothing to do with money. That's life. And that's what relationships are built on—the trust that you have knowing that we care about you and your family and your progress.

Have quick access. Ever been on hold for 10 minutes, 20, 30, or more? And had to listen to that annoying electronic music that can burn a hole in your eardrum? Yeah, me too. And I can't stand it. Too bad that's common practice for many large companies. With a firm like ours, you'll get quick access to advisors when you call the office. (Our business model is about serving you well with depth and care, not about serving thousands of people and barely serving them at all.) The point is this: when you have a problem or concern, you need to know you can get to someone promptly, so we make it easy for you to do that.

No question is too weird. You wouldn't believe some of the questions I've gotten serving as a fiduciary. I've fielded inquiries about everything from economic to what to do about children who are living in the basement after college or are spinning their wheels in college with no direction. All of it is fair game, and our job is to help our clients get solutions and navigate tricky waters (we've seen it all, and we often have just the recommendation to help. If we don't, we'll research it). You can imagine that early on, it might feel odd to tell your fiduciary that you are in a pickle with your spouse about how to spend a year-end bonus because you really, really, really want a new [fill in the blank with your vice that causes arguments with your spouse]. But over time that trust builds and builds, and you realize that a good fiduciary won't judge you; we only want to help you.

Honesty above all else. For this relationship to work in the short and long term, there's one key ingredient, and that's honesty. We pledge to be honest with you, even if the truth hurts (no, you can't afford the sailboat right now, but let's work on ways to get one within three years). So in return we need you to be straightforward with us.

When all of this works together, you get the final result: a firm that has a team of people with complementary skill sets and specialties who are on call for you to help you navigate and leap over the hurdles in life. I'm proud to say that many, many of our clients have become good friends. How many people can say that about a robotic voice on the other end of the phone when you're trying to talk to someone about changing your 401K allocations? Not too many. Not too many at all.

The Wealth Management Business

As you know by now, a lot of what a quality fiduciary firm will do are the things that other firms don't. But make no mistake, we know one of your major concerns: How much will your money grow? And while the answer can never be guaranteed, we absolutely do consider wealth management a major aspect of what we do. After all, part of securing time and freedom is also securing your money. Four quick examples:

We Help You Think Differently. Many of the successful investors that we meet are of the opinion that they need to be prepared to call it quits at work at age 65. This has become the American way as the transition into retirement. This idea is antiquated and encourages sedentary behavior on some of the most promising years of your life. You have experience on your side and a wealth of knowledge that you have built over the years. Hopefully you have kept in good shape and are committed to living a healthy, exciting, and productive next chapter in your life. What we see here is that a mindset shift is essential to continue living your active vibrant professional life in new and creative ways. Perhaps you decide to work part-time as a consultant. Or could also change fields completely and take on a new challenge. Or you could partner with one of your children (if you are so blessed) and bring your wisdom to the table with their enthusiasm and creativity to make a go in an entirely new business. Our view is that your fiduciary firm should help you with doing the research to succeed at your new venture.

Diversify, Diversify, Diversify. Many investors get hung up on the idea of finding the best stock out there and staking their future on that stock purchase decision. Since I've never met anyone with a crystal ball, we, like many fiduciaries, mentor our client to thoroughly diversify their portfolios. As technology has expanded, the systems to diversify have become increasingly more effective. With sufficient funds you can buy direct indexed portfolios which rebalance every trading day. The advantage to you, the investor, is significant as these direct indexed portfolios allow for more effective tax loss harvesting and keep more money in your pocket. A good fiduciary can take this approach and assemble other ETFs, mutual funds, or individual securities to support your portfolios to achieve the stability or growth you want. Over time, as you hone in on the family priorities you have, your fiduciary will help you achieve your family's goals.

Big Firm vs. Boutique Firm. Which one serves in your best interest? Your big box firms are well equipped but often lack personal touch. Small firms can sometimes offer you the TLC that you may desire but may not be well equipped with the latest sophisticated technology. You want to make sure your fiduciary advisor is both well-equipped and excels at providing the personal touch. A good fiduciary will have access to all the important investment-analysis tools—such as Bloomberg, Y Charts, eMoney, and other programs that you may have heard of.

Alternative Ways of Raising Funds: When the need for money arises, we look seriously at alternative ways of raising funds. What are they? Borrowing money depends on the time horizon of how long you will need the money. You could of course use a line of credit at the bank. You must recognize that due to the amount of paperwork and committee approvals, there could be significant time delays and costs with that line of credit. If the amount needed is modest, say $50,000 - $100,000 you may consider searching out a zero percent interest rate credit card for the 6 to 12 month period of time offered. A smarter way to borrow may be to find a HELOC (Home Equity Line of Credit) which could provide tax benefits as well as an attractive rate. Finally there are margin borrowing opportunities available at your favorite custodian or brokerage firm which may have significantly lower interest rates with potential tax benefits as well. You get quick access to funds without liquidating your current assets and it provides a source of funds with repayment flexibility, so you can use it for personal financial needs (like emergency expenses, tuition, home purchase, debt consolidation, and other needs).

Chapter 10

THE SWEETEST VICTORIES

**How a good fiduciary can help you solve
the most common financial conflicts.**

To tweak a phrase from Forrest Gump: life is like a box of conflicts.
It's true. Everywhere you turn you see conflicts of all kinds. You've got
the big ones, like wars. You've got the small ones, like not agreeing what
show to binge-watch on Netflix. And you've got a whole range of ones
in between, including ones that nag on you (like family troubles), ones
that are simply annoying (not getting the contractor to finish the job),
ones that have serious consequences (legal trouble), and ones that don't
ever seem to have a solution (insert your own hefty dilemma here). I'd
be naive to think that you can just wash away conflicts like stains from
a shirt. Conflicts are part of life, and in many ways working through
our troubles is one of the ways we grow and get stronger and smarter.

But let's also be clear: life is too short to have troubles weighing you
down 24/7. You've got things to do, people to love, sports and games
to play, work to finish, and passions to pursue. So the more time you

spend with pounding headaches as you work out your problems, the less time you have to do with life what you've always dreamed of doing.

And that's where we come in. As I hope you've seen from all the information in this book, a high-quality fiduciary wears many hats, but perhaps the largest one of all is the role of Conflict Solver. We aim to make life easier for you by finding answers—or finding the right people who can give you answers.

Here I'll take you through some of the most common financially related conflicts I have seen in my three decades of serving clients and show you what we do to solve them. This chapter focuses on people who are a bit older—either they have firmly established themselves or are close to retirement, while the next chapter takes a look at some common questions I get from clients who are more in the just-getting-started phase of life.

Dear Irvin,

I have one adult child who really has her act together. She's financially independent, manages her money well, and never asks for anything. I have another child who hasn't always found his way, has struggled at times, and has needed our help. I love them both dearly, of course. How do I handle the balance financially between helping one child while still trying to be fair to both?

—Robert

Oftentimes our clients run into major dilemmas about how they support children and still divide up their money fairly, especially when it involves family members in need. What if one child or grandchild needs money? Remember the story I told you about the grandchild who was in college debt and had a drug problem? The grandparents wanted to help; they really, really wanted to. But they also were keenly aware that paying off a student loan and paying for rehab was an extraordinary expense—and a gift that wouldn't be equally valued among all the children and grandchildren. Where we came in was to be the quarterback and then the scorekeeper—an impartial party that could track the money that the grandfather gave to his child and grandchild, so that it could be deducted from the grandchildren's inheritance and ensure fair distribution of assets upon the passing of the grandparents. We see this issue frequently, especially when it comes to families. So often one child is the one who really needs extra help, putting the patriarch and matriarch in the uncomfortable position of trying to help that child, but not at the expense of the other children.

That same principle extends toward business as well. I have a doctor client named John, who shared a practice with three other doctors. John wanted to scale back his hours, but the other partners thought that along with the scaling back of hours should come the scaling back of pay. How did they work it out so everything was fair? We looked at all the numbers, made suggestions, and negotiated the terms of such a deal. While we of course represented John, we worked with the emotional baggage that arose when the three doctors tried to work it out themselves.

These scenarios are very common, very real, and very frustrating. That's why we're there to look at all sides of a situation and work to come up with solutions. Part of our role is to solve family problems (or find effective compromises) early on to facilitate family communication and the relationship, because if the problems are not handled, they will fester and get worse and worse.

One of the common ways we handle a situation when you're helping a child in need is to use the money earmarked for inheritance, so any present-time distributions are deducted from what the family member might receive in an inheritance. It levels the playing field, albeit in different periods of your life, while tracking each child's distributions along the way.

> Dear Irvin,
>
> I've made a lot of money in my career, and I do well for myself and my family. I have plenty saved for retirement, and I do want to do exactly what you're recommending—accomplish the things in life that I want and enjoy my life with my family. So here's the deal: I want to buy a vacation home. I want to host my adult children (and their children) and make it a regular part of our lives together. I'm looking at a variety of loans. And, wow, there are a lot of options! What do you typically recommend?
>
> —Nancy

When you have a fair amount of money, it's not uncommon for you to want even more money to do something grander (hello, beach house) or for others, especially in your family, to ask you for money. And if you're in the place where you can make that move, that can be a wonderful investment for your enjoyment—and to use "something" to connect all of the important "someones" in your life.

Loans can be tricky business, between the terms, the taxes, the interest rates, and the repayment arrangements. Why do you have to figure it all out? You don't. We'll take a look at all the options and come up with best recommendations for whatever your need is. And we'll also look at the passion that drives this—does this include multiple generations or just the couple?

Here's one example. A client of ours, Ken, wanted to purchase a country house for his family. The problem was that Ken's main source of income came from a large trust fund set up by his parents, and a bank would not give him a fair interest rate on a mortgage. Ken's father had died, and his mom was still the trustee of the trust. Given that interest rates for "intra-family" loans were at their all-time lows, we advised our client that the best outcome would be to ask the trustee if he could borrow from the trust to purchase the house. His mom agreed, and the loan was structured so that he would have to pay "interest only" for 10 years on the loan, and the loan could be extended another 10 years if the trustee agreed to continue the loan. If his mom died within the first 10 years, he would have inherited the trust outright and could pay off the loan at any time.

It's also important to note that what we find in many cases is that when looking at a vacation home, people care less about the logistics than they do about what it means. They don't care if the rooms or beds are small or the kitchen isn't as perfect as they would want; they just want a place for the family—and many generations—to come together to laugh, to play, to make memories. But that doesn't mean the financial questions aren't important. In fact that's why fiduciaries can be so vital; we do the heavy lifting, so our clients can dream their dreams and we can drill down the details.

As we would do in any similar situation, we didn't just suggest the intra-family loan as the only option. We also looked at bank alternatives, like traditional financing and other kinds of trust loans. We crunched the numbers, looked at all the variables, and came up with what worked best for our client. The same answer wouldn't apply to everyone, which is why those initial steps—learning about your values, goals, and priorities—are so crucial to establishing a long-term relationship with your fiduciary. Many of our decisions are about money, of course, but they'll also be considered in context of everything else happening in your life. When it comes to such things as your financial means, your time horizons, your risk parameters, taxes, family-fairness issues, and other related issues we look to you for the proper priority to get to the finish line.

Dear Irvin,

Confession time: I know all the advice, and I knew better. But my spouse and I didn't put away as much for retirement as we should have, and now I feel like we're behind. I'm in my late 50s and when I try to crunch the numbers myself, I feel like I wouldn't be able to stop working until I'm 80 or something! I know I can't take back time, but is there something else I can do to catch up on my retirement?

—Gerry

You can make the case that this is one of the most fundamental personal problems with lifestyles today. So many people fail to save early enough (throughout their lives when dollar-cost averaging will really make your money grow), and they're stuck wanting to retire but not having the means to do so. They live in the moment, they live above their means, and they live for the now instead of for the future.

Many years ago a couple named Fred and Ethel came to us with just under $750,000 saved. Their joint income was more than $600,000 a year, but they overspent—on everything except their retirement accounts. Fred and Ethel came to us saying they wanted to retire at 55. Using our advanced cash flow planning software, we showed them what comes in, what goes out, and what goes to Uncle Sam. The math didn't add up. If they retired at 55, they would be broke by 60. Not much of a shocker. By going back to the drawing board and having Fred and Ethel eliminate unnecessary "wants," they started first with the basics (paying yourself first in order to save then cutting back on unnecessary expenses). That savings mentality developed into maximizing their retirement plan contributions each year and dollar-cost averaging into a joint taxable account. Fifteen years later, our client who began with $750,000 saved to $4 million saved for retirement (after lifestyle expenses). That's the power of saving and compound interest at work. In these cases, we can make money grow, but we need two things from them—time and their commitment to live within their means and contribute to their investments on a regular and consistent basis.

> Dear Irvin,
> I've always taken care of my own portfolio. I manage my investments, and I even play with some day-trading from time to time. I feel like I've done pretty well for myself, as I do a lot of reading and learning about markets and various kinds of investments. Is that really a bad thing for me to do on my own?
> —Grace

Do it yourself investing doesn't have to be a bad thing, but you should be aware of some common pitfalls. Many of them tend to chase the hot dot. This means that they invest in whatever is doing the best at the moment. They will often buy near the high price for a stock, and when it begins to sell off, they get nervous and sell that same investment. Then they buy the next hot investment, which provides for mediocre returns over time. Others think they know exactly how to invest their wealth, or maybe they're afraid to make any changes to the tactics they've used for years. You may want to check out my earlier book *Reinvent Rich: How to Make More Money, More Moments and*

More Meaning in Life, for in depth insights on best investing techniques (See Chapter 5).

We had a business couple, Linda and Jay, join our firm as clients many years ago. Linda and Jay worked for a large publicly traded health-care company (where they met), and they had high-paying jobs and were enmeshed in the cultural identity of the company. Over the course of their careers, they had amassed millions of dollars of publicly traded stock and stock options. They joined us in need of guidance because the company's stock price became volatile, and they could no longer take the ride because their time horizon to retirement was getting nearer.

From our detailed analysis, we were able to demonstrate to Linda and Jay that a diversified portfolio is better positioned to withstand when the stock market becomes volatile. We embarked on a multiyear plan of selling the stock each year by setting a capital gains budget to minimize taxes. We set price targets to maximize the profits of their stock options and set up a charitable donor-advised fund to donate highly appreciated shares to go to their charitable endeavors which further reduced their tax exposure. Fast forward many years later, and they still own the stock in their portfolio, but in much smaller quantities and have a diversified portfolio—which creates a much more resilient portfolio for them in the long run. Ultimately, as you saw in the previous chapter, we're here to maximize your wealth and minimize your risk, which is why wealth management is such an integral part of our approach and focus.

> Dear Irvin,
>
> I got divorced about 10 years ago when my children were in high school. I have good relationships with them and even my ex-spouse. Well, a few years ago, I met someone who I fell in love with, and I am getting remarried again. I'm very happy, and I have a lot of trust in my new spouse, but I also know the realities of second marriages. My main concern is making sure my adult children are protected. What are my best options?
>
> —Daniel

First off, a big congrats to you and your new spouse-to-be, Daniel! We have had many clients who get married well into their Golden Years. We even had one client, my dear friend Leonard, get married well into his 80s. Now the last thing we would want a client of ours to do is jump into a new life-changing event without checking all of the boxes. We make sure our clients know all of the marriage planning alternatives available.

For example, a prenuptial agreement is one method that clients can protect themselves and their adult children with when entering into a second marriage (especially important for high-wealth clients). We also look at beneficiary designations, whether that be on life insurance policies or retirement accounts, to ensure assets that you want to pass down to your kids go to them and not inadvertently to a second spouse. Finally, updating your estate documents is the best way to ensure your kids inherit what you want them to receive. This doesn't mean you have to cut out your new spouse from your will. Your new spouse might have sufficient assets that he or she doesn't need your money. If you still want to take care of your spouse after you're gone and still leave the "farm" for your kids, we often see this carried out with a trust. One such trust is called a QTIP or Qualified Terminable Interest Property Trust. With this type of trust, you are setting aside a chunk of your estate from which your spouse can be entitled to income every year while preserving the principal for future generations, i.e., your kids and grandkids.

Dear Irvin,

I've done all the right things in terms of saving, creating strong retirement funds, and even having an emergency account. But frankly I'm scared to death of a financial emergency—like if something happens to my spouse, who is the main breadwinner in the family. How do I prepare?

—Joan

That's a very real problem—and a scary one. Certainly some emergencies depend on your current financial situation and how you and your spouse have set up your liquidity fund as well as your portfolio allocations. Thoughtful meetings with your fiduciary team should include not only financial planning but healthcare planning as well. Our goal is to make sure you are taken care of. We had one client, Mary Beth, whose husband died suddenly of a heart attack. Mary Beth had no adviser and modest liquid assets. Their net worth was in a handful of residential real estate properties that paid them income. Maintenance was minimal because the husband did all the property management. Over several years we worked with Mary Beth to sell the real estate to create a portfolio of liquid assets to support her lifestyle (in the meantime we did hire a person to act as property manager, since her husband did all that work and found her a trustworthy virtual administrative assistant to help pay her daily bills). After all the properties were sold (including her personal residence), she moved to a low-maintenance condo. She has been living off her portfolio comfortably ever since.

In summary, since life changing events are often unexpected, the bottom line is that we can help figure out the best course for any situation. You're smart to ask now—because being prepared is much better than struggling at the last minute.

> Dear Irvin,
>
> I'm nearing retirement age. And I'm torn about a lot. I'm afraid of losing my identity. I don't know what I should be doing—I don't even know if it's the right thing to retire. Now don't get me wrong—I'm looking forward to more sleep and more free time, but I'm not exactly raring to go for retirement. What's your best advice for someone in my situation?
>
> —Raymond

I'm so glad you asked that, Raymond, because it's actually a very common question. Retirement can be a wonderful thing, but it can be scarier than a top-notch horror flick. When you ask that question, it reminds me of my friend and client, Kenneth. Well, when he retired as a lawyer, you know what he told me years after retirement? He said that while he loved his career, he was having the most fun of his life right now—in his 80s—writing poetry! And that's not even mentioning that he's finishing up writing a book too. Poetry and tending his garden are his true passions. He is living a fulfilling life focusing on what he loves to do most. My advice in this arena comes down to four things:

- Make sure you are indeed financially secure and have the means to support the life you want. We can help crunch the numbers and make sure you have the connections you need to succeed.
- Live your passions. This is the time to do more of what you want. You just have to do it. Nothing is holding you back now!
- Connect with younger folks. One of the best ways to stay young is to surround yourself with lots of young energetic people. You may find them in your neighborhood, in volunteering, in areas that you believe in, engaging in your hobbies or interests that you are passionate about, or memory building activities with your family. Remember, as a more mature person, you bring the wisdom and experience. They bring the fire in their belly and lots of energy. It's a win-win for all parties.
- Don't stop if you don't want to. Many people find fulfilling postretirement careers that don't have to revolve around just making a buck. It could be volunteering at a museum or something that aligns your passions with helping others to keep you young and vital.

Dear Irvin,

I'm going crazy, between the price of gas and the price of real estate and the price of about near everything. Inflation is really getting to me. How do I keep up?

—Elizabeth

Inflation is the silent destroyer of wealth. I get this question all the time with clients and friends. The best method to stay ahead of inflation is to conduct a thorough search to find a trustworthy fiduciary advisory firm to work with you and your family. The goal is to develop a diverse portfolio of assets to deal with the ravages of inflation. It's worth the time and effort to have a firm that will be your advocate and will partner with you to deal with the changing economic developments around the world.

> Dear Irvin,
> I'm at the age where I can start taking Social Security. I've read about advantages and disadvantages to signing up for it at different times. When do you suggest someone takes Social Security?
> —Michael

Your decision comes down to several key factors Michael: outside income streams and longevity are your primary questions. Uncle Sam allows you to start taking Social Security retirement benefits once you turn age 62. However, you might want to think twice about doing that because your benefit will be reduced by 7-8% for each year you start claiming benefits before full retirement age (FRA). Currently, FRA is age 66 or 67 depending upon when you were born.

Getting back to your question, Michael, if you have retirement accounts, a taxable account, a pension, or savings in the bank to live off until FRA, that's often your best route. If you want to truly maximize SS benefits, the latest you can wait to claim benefits is age 70. For every year you wait beyond FRA, your benefits grow by 8 percent. In terms of longevity, if living a long, prosperous life runs in the family, you might want to consider claiming at age 70 since you will be getting your highest benefit. On the flip side, if everyone in the family has passed on by age 80, you might want to claim your benefits at your FRA. A note to remember: if you do wait until age 70 to claim SS benefits, Uncle Sam won't magically start sending you checks the month of your 70th birthday. You still need to call your local Social Security office or go online to start the benefit claiming process.

Chapter 11

YOUNG AND BOLD

**Especially when you're starting out, it's important
to make smart financial decisions.**

If you are at a certain age or stage in life, you might think that the word
"fiduciary" sounds as foreign as arrivederci.

And that's understandable. Many people when they're starting out
don't think much about their financial futures. They may not have
much money, may not make a lot of money—or they're the opposite:
their families have been wealthy, so they assume there's nothing for
them to worry about.

The reality is that no matter what end of the spectrum you're on—
or somewhere in the middle—it's never too early to start to strategize
about your wealth and begin your wealth creation. After all, the number-one thing you can do for your future is to save now. But that's just
the start of it.

Young people have lots of questions about what to do, how to spend,
how to save, and how to navigate financial conflicts and questions that

are specific to their own age group. Here's a sample of some of the more common scenarios we hear—and how we work through them.

> Dear Irvin,
>
> I just received a large inheritance from a relative. I know it sounds like I'm being spoiled because I'm lucky enough to benefit, but it's not like I want to buy a Bentley or take an around-the-world cruise or something. I'm just overwhelmed by it all.
>
> What do I do?
>
> —Jason

First of all, I'm very sorry for your loss, Jason. That makes the situation much harder, but your problem—at least financially—is a good one to have in that your inheritance can give you some security and stability for your future. The reality is that inheritance, especially if you aren't used to handling a lot of money, can be an intimidating challenge. What should you do? How should you spend it? What gets taxed? How can you protect as much as possible?

We often see clients who inherit a lot of money become fearful when deciding how to best move forward with managing this newfound wealth. A recent client of ours, Emma, came to us after inheriting a few million dollars from the passing of her father and her aunt. In her inheritance Emma received legacy stocks that had been underperforming the market for years and U.S. savings bonds. The savings bonds were so old that some bonds had been matured for years and stopped accruing interest. When asked why she never cashed the bonds in, her reply was that she was afraid to pay the taxes. We completed a tax analysis that showed her that by selling the matured or low-interest savings bonds over a period of years, she could smooth out the tax bite from Uncle Sam. In addition we also set a capital gains tax budget to facilitate selling her inherited underperforming equities. Having a solid plan in place gave her newfound confidence. Now she makes better financial decisions, enjoys more wealth, and lives a happier life.

In another client example, a couple named Bill and Lucy had a large windfall and needed a plan. We immediately took action: we paid down over $160,000 in student debt from their children's college education. The debt burden was growing and would have turned into well over a $200,000 obligation since their children were still in college. Then we refinanced the mortgage to a lower rate and reduced the term to 15 years to pay it down faster while mortgage rates were low. We also maximized retirement contributions to increase net worth and reduce taxes. We connected Bill and Lucy with an accountant to assist in making sure they were getting all the deductions they deserved.

Without our help and the windfall, it could have been a disaster. By their own admission, they may have gone bankrupt trying to figure out all the moving pieces.

Dear Irvin,

I'm newly married and so happy. I'm also fairly new in my career (about five years in), and my spouse and I are talking about starting a family. We've rented an apartment all our lives, but we're now debating about the next step. Should we rent or buy?

—Thomas

This is a question we get from clients of all age demographics. The answer to this one, like most financial planning questions, is "it depends." If you're working in a new city for a short period of time (let's say 18 months or shorter), it's probably a good idea to bite the bullet and rent. If you're planning on working in a new location for longer than three years, it's probably better to consider buying a home if you have the available liquidity. We also see this question pop up for a lot of our clients who retire and want to move to a more warm and friendly location. It's preferable to rent for six months or even a year when first moving to a different part of the country. This way you can get the lay of the land. Do we like the people? Is it too hot in the summer? Does Dennis the Menace live next door? You definitely want to answer these questions first before making a large commitment like buying a house.

> Dear Irvin,
> OK, I'll just say it. I'm confused about mortgages, like are fixed or adjustable mortgages better? I don't understand the differences.
> —Paul

I get these questions a lot from folks who have committed to the decision of buying a house. For your first question, my usual answer is it more than likely comes down to time horizon. If you are only going to be in your home for a few years (10 or fewer years), then it's usually best to go with an adjustable-rate mortgage (ARM). ARMs are very similar to fixed-rate mortgages in that they are fixed for a period such as 5, 7, or 10 years. Then at the end of the period, the interest rate adjusts to the going market interest rate with caps. These types of mortgages are most attractive because the interest rate is lower during the locked in period than a traditional fixed mortgage. Fixed rate mortgages do serve a purpose, especially if you think you've found your forever home or if you believe interest rates will increase in the future. In those cases, a 15-year or 30-year fixed mortgage might be the right choice for you and your family.

Dear Irvin,

I have two toddlers, and I know that finishing high school is a long way away—though everyone tells me it'll go by really fast! I want to start saving for my children's college costs early. I know it's the right thing to do. How do I start?

—Alyssa

The best time to start investing was always yesterday, but it's never too late to start today. A 529 plan is a fantastic option to save for college funds. These plans are state-sponsored education accounts that allow you to start saving for college with tax-free growth. Some states even offer you a tax deduction off your personal income tax return. So long as you use the funds for "qualified education expenses" like tuition, books, room and board, equipment, etc., distributions from 529 plans are tax free.

To start all you need is your child's social security number to make them the beneficiary. Parents don't even need to set up these plans. They can be established by grandparents, uncles, aunts, or cousins. If monies remain in your child's 529 plan after they've graduated, all is not lost. The funds can be transferred to another child or remain in the account to continue to grow for your kid's children. When choosing a 529 plan, review state plans that have low-cost investment options. High-expense ratio investment options chip away at long-term returns. If you want to put investing on "autopilot", consider a glide path option. Glide path investment portfolios start out nearly 100 percent in stocks when your child is young and rebalance every year on your child's birthday, becoming less aggressive until it's time to go to college. Remember, you aren't wedded to your state's 529 plan. If it is inferior, you can choose another state! These are important decisions to review with your fiduciary ahead of time.

Dear Irvin,

I've started a new job, and the benefits seem really strong, though it's hard for me to know for sure. My health insurance plan offers a Health Savings Account (HSA). That's good, right?

—Alexander

HSA accounts are what I like to call the fourth bucket in a retirement plan that goes along with pretax retirement, Roth accounts, and after-tax individual accounts. A health savings account is a type of financial account where participants are allowed to contribute dollars that go toward healthcare expenses.

To have one of these accounts, you *must* have a high-deductible health plan. If you don't have a high-deductible health plan, you are not allowed to contribute. HSAs offer triple tax benefits. First, you get a tax deduction for employee contributions each year. Second, these accounts offer a brokerage account feature, so if you invest your contributions in the markets, the growth is tax free over time. Third, distributions for "qualified medical expenses" (e.g., doctor visits, copays, prescriptions, etc.) are tax free. Be careful, because if you take a distribution for non-medical expenses, the IRS makes you pay ordinary income tax on the distribution, and a penalty may apply if you are under the age of 65. HSAs do have a neat little perk worth mentioning once you get to age 65. You may take distributions from your HSA for non-qualified medical expenses without being subject to a penalty; however, ordinary income tax would still apply. In a sense it's like having an additional IRA account in retirement.

• • •

As you can see from these various case studies, each of these people struggled with uncertainty about handling their circumstances in relation to the problems they were dealing with in their lives. It was problematic in each case because they didn't have sufficient information nor experience in coping with their changing lives. This is where a fiduciary can be irreplaceable.

A fiduciary provides peace of mind and a logical approach in an emotional climate. As you experience yourself, human beings are emotional creatures (we see that again and again, whether we're watching sports or political battles over on Facebook!). That emotion comes in handy sometimes, but it can also cloud our decision making when the logical side of our brains should take over but doesn't.

Let's take a common example: when it comes to money and investments, our tendency is to wait until markets are doing well and going up in order to invest. Makes emotional sense, right? Things are good; it's a good time to get into the game—let's do it! But as the markets are going up, the ship may have already sailed, and things tend to level out, meaning that there's not as much potential for growth.

What happens in the opposite scenario? Say there's political unrest, or you have health issues, or there's a change in the federal administration, or inflation is starting to rear its ugly head, or there are wartime scenarios? People—feeling the instability in the world around them—tend to run for the exits and put their money in gold, treasuries, or some sort of other asset that feels safe and gives them comfort.

But when things get painful, that's often the best time to jump in.

And that's where we come in. A good firm can help you deploy your capital in stages. Nobody knows when the bottom will be there (everybody tries to figure it out), but a fiduciary firm will help you invest smartly and deal with the emotion. Our experience seeing what markets do and how they react serves as the yin (logic) to your yang (emotion), and that's a good thing. Bringing decades of experience to these volatile markets, we can hold your hand and give you peace of mind.

Making the right balance of investments at the right time is the best way to allocate portfolios to make more money. And if you don't have the stomach for it, a fiduciary firm can help negate your nausea. By being very clear about what we're doing and why we're doing it, we give the confidence to make the best decisions with you and your family.

Chapter 12

MAKE YOUR HARD WORK WORK FOR YOU

A traditional financial advisor isn't enough, reach for more.

By now you should have a good idea of what a partnership focused fiduciary can provide to successful families in this game called life. You may think from your experience with your own financial advisor that helping you invest money is simple and easy and nothing more than routine. In our experience, that attitude doesn't work. After decades of experience with many individuals and families, we have developed these essential conclusions:

You are different from everybody else.

Your family situation and level of communication is different from everybody else's.

Your goals are different from everybody else's.

Your time horizons are different from everybody else's.

Your passions in life are different from everybody else's.

Your day-to-day lifestyle, with all of the moving parts, is different from everybody else's.

Your portfolios, liquidity, and personal needs are different from everybody else's.

As you can see, true wealth management is not like a rain poncho—one size does *not* fit all. Wealth creation and preservation are about diving deep into your inner being and figuring out what will work for you.

As we near the end of the book, it's important to realize that even if the differences I mentioned above don't apply to you, the bigger point is that you have or will have increasing demands on your time and money, especially as you accumulate more wealth.

Yes, you could navigate some of these things on your own, but that's like sailing around the world with no crew, no GPS, and a storm approaching. There are going to be some rough seas ahead.

Isn't it better to have a crew that can help, radar to warn you of storms, and a vessel that can get you to safe and clear waters?

That's what a good fiduciary is all about: smooth sailing.

One other important note: if you are your family steward and now using a good fiduciary firm, this is an amazing opportunity—and even responsibility—to pass along some of the estate planning lessons to your children. We recommend getting them involved as early as you are comfortable in the process. Get them aligned with your family goals. Get them aligned with our fiduciary firm to help uphold your family values and to help them on their own savings and wealth creation techniques.

We are at an amazing point in history. For one, this generation will see more growth in wealth than ever before. Why? Because the heirs of the Boomer generation stand to inherit trillions of dollars. And those heirs will not always know what to do and how to handle the complexities that come with sudden wealth. Second, we're also in a very unusual time when the stresses of life seem overwhelming. People are confused, people are under pressure, and people have a lot more stress than they feel like they can handle.

And that is a dangerous course: opportunity and anxiety can create a tornado of tumult.

That's where we come in. We can foresee problems. We can fix problems. We can think through problems. And we can give you exactly what this book is all about.

More time.

More money.

More freedom.

You deserve more from life. We can help you get it.

The Cheat Sheet for Your Perfect Partnership

- Find a fiduciary firm that's small and nimble enough to be your trusted advocate and help your family create wealth and avoid the stumbling blocks of life.
- Make time to meet with your fiduciary advocates to uncover the dangers, opportunities, and strengths that your family is dealing with.
- Develop a first-year plan with your top three priorities to achieve success (for you, your children, and your extended family, if applicable).
- Make sure to set aside cash reserves for an emergency.
- Teach your family to have the courage to save intelligently and see the benefits of disciplined investing.
- Create wealth by setting boundaries beginning with dollar-cost averaging and not deviating when the market becomes volatile.
- Remember, your goal is not to save everything, but to be a committed saver and set up a budget for fun to enjoy your life.
- Be ready to change as your life changes—and prepare to see the benefit for your entire extended family.
- Stretch your fiduciary firm to help you in other important areas of life, utilizing their professional network to connect you to the solution providers, vendors, or services that can reduce the stress in your life.

Appendix

RESOURCES FOR YOUR FAMILY

Life Changing Next Steps

What You Should Do for You

The bulk of this book is about what a fiduciary firm can do for you, but I hope you haven't missed the parts where I point to what you can do to help yourself. After all, when it comes down to it, the responsibility is yours when it comes to deciding what actions to ultimately take. In addition I do feel very strongly that the people who take personal responsibility have a better handle on life—and life's curveballs. To that end I have worked with many people over the last thirty years, and I can tell you that the ones with the healthiest habits are the ones who usually come out better on the other end. While everybody's lives and circumstances are certainly different, I have observed patterns over the years, and these are the good habits I find are common to the most successful people.

Family:

- Develop a strong, grounded, supportive family environment.
- Teach children your family values.
- Hold family meetings, whether they be monthly or quarterly, to talk about goals.
- Teach children the value of a dollar.
- Read every day. There's always an opportunity to learn something new.
- Spend less time watching TV and on your phone. Do more family activities together.

Financial:

- Save at least 10% of your monthly income.
- Pay yourself first before paying for "expenses or wants."
- Have a fully funded emergency account for a minimum of 6 months.
- Minimize non-tax deductible debt.
- Pay your credit cards off monthly.
- Limit spending on wasteful "wants."
- Indulge on experiences with family, not big-ticket items.

Life:

- Have your estate planning documents in order (i.e., wills, trusts, POAs).
- Designate beneficiaries for your retirement accounts and life insurance policies.

- Have insurance to cover all your bases: life, home, auto, disability, umbrella.

ACKNOWLEDGEMENT

As I began writing "Who's On Your Dream Team", I was very inspired by the concept of what distinguished a fiduciary advisor from other financial advisors, and how the nuances of each made an enormous difference in how clients are served. Strong fiduciary teams create partnerships significantly different than financial advisors who manage a book of business. This delineation is at the core of why I wrote this book.

I have a strong desire to thank those who have been in my inner circle and supported my efforts to clarify these important distinctions. Many people have helped me in my goal to educate those in search of insights and support as they work to extend their lives and their money, for themselves and their families.

My special thanks to Ted Spiker, who is my co-writer on both of my books on how to maximize your life through the lens of money and finance. Ted introduced me to George Karabotsos and his creative skills with graphic design which have been most helpful.

Two members of our Pennsylvania Capital Management Team, Andrew Randisi and Christopher Mallon helped in this endeavor with contributions to the financial content.

Steve Poulathas gave freely of his time to discuss nuances from an estate planning and legal perspective and encouraged me to explore and expand concepts essential to serving families.

My gratitude to Mehmet Oz and Mike Roizen for their detailed and constructive insights on stress reduction and steps to extend longevity. Additionally, I extend my appreciation to Ben duPont, Skip DiMassa and Lee Brower for their ongoing insights and clear direction as this book was developed. My conversations with all of these experts over the years have contributed so much to my view of helping families build a bigger future.

No one has been more important to me in the pursuit of this project than the members of my family. I would like to thank my parents, Anita and Irvin Schorsch, who taught me that everyday counts, including my Dad's advice to fly a flag that has one word on it – TODAY! Most importantly, I wish to thank my loving and supportive wife, Marilyn, and my three wonderful children, Stephanie, Garrett and Merrie, who provide unending support and inspiration.

ABOUT THE AUTHOR

Irvin Schorsch

In 1995, Irvin Schorsch founded Pennsylvania Capital Management with the entrepreneurial vision to build a firm centered on the client first and foremost and to help people crystallize their thinking about the future of their lives and financial goals.

Irvin represents a new breed of wealth advisors who are passionate about providing the highest level of personalized service and attention. He's committed to developing a life-long, multi-generational relationship with our clients. This involves gaining a deeper understanding of family dynamics, their spending habits and the nuances of how individuals, couples and private business owners approach and prepare for major milestones and transitions.

Irvin is the ultimate optimist and the visionary of Pennsylvania Capital Management. He believes that with enough effort, the right level of commitment, and an understanding of what the finish line looks like, people can achieve virtually anything. He is also acutely attuned to identifying changing expectations that require reformulating and establishing new goals. He challenges clients to achieve a richer, fuller life with a greater sense of purpose. Together they develop new ways of creating wealth along with life planning strategies to help them realize their financial hopes and dreams.

Irvin graduated with honors from the Commerce and Finance Division of Villanova University. He has earned three advanced certifications: Certified Financial Planner™ from the College for Financial Planning in Denver, Colorado; the Certified Investment Management Analyst SM designation through the Wharton School of the University of Pennsylvania in conjunction with the Investment Management Consultants Association; and the Accredited Investment Fiduciary® awarded by the Center for Fiduciary Studies, which is associated with the University of Pittsburgh.

Irvin is an in-demand author, speaker, and consultant on many topics from financial planning to wealth management for all demographics and age groups. Mr. Schorsch can be reached at 215-881-7700 or irvin@pcmadvisors.com.

www.ingramcontent.com/pod-product-compliance
Lightning Source LLC
Chambersburg PA
CBHW050512210326
41521CB00011B/2431